INVESTING STRATEGIES FOR ADULTS

EFFECTIVE WAYS OF MAKING A PROFIT WITH LOW-RISK INVESTMENTS. WORKING JUST 1 HOUR A DAY WITH LITTLE OR NO EXPERIENCE

T.D. MATTHEW

CONTENTS

INTRODUCTION

Without a doubt, one of the things that people yearn for the most is to achieve financial freedom and thus be unconcerned about everything that has to do with money. Unfortunately, the vast majority of people do not know how to accomplish that long-awaited financial freedom. Did you know that you could make more than $10,000 over the next five years with zero work simply by skipping Starbucks and investing that "extra" $5.00 each day instead? This is because most of the things that will help people achieve success in their personal finances are fundamental issues that are directly related to their daily habits. That is why, by changing certain financial habits, learning about investments, and mastering your emotions, you will be able to turn your finances around in order to achieve that lifestyle you have always wanted and never have to worry about money again. Most people believe that it is impossible to reach the status of a millionaire or that they have to work all their lives to survive. However, you should know that through intelligent investments, you can achieve a lifestyle where you make money even when you are asleep. Millionaires and people who have been successful in the world of investments know that the key is making money work for them, while most people think they must work for money.

That is why, throughout this book, you will learn some of the fundamental concepts involved in the world of investments and all those financial habits you must acquire to achieve a stable economic position and begin to plan your future the way you want. You must always remember that investments are important not only to improve your current financial situation but also very important for the future since these are the ones in charge of allowing you to have a quiet retirement where money is not an issue. What happens to many people when they reach retirement age is that, even though they have worked all their lives, have always paid their taxes, and have maintained exemplary behaviour in society, they do not have enough savings to live the lifestyle they want. This is something that happens in every country in the world, and it is worrying to see how schools and the entire educational system have not been in charge of guiding people on all these topics. Many people believe that the world of investments is reserved only for economists, accountants, or financial advisors. Still, the truth is that anyone can aspire to invest intelligently and thus multiply their savings and create an excellent monetary base for their future—one of the most important things you should do in your life.

Investments can often seem very difficult and even almost impossible to carry out successfully. However, little by little, you will realize that it is straightforward to invest effectively without the need to have a lot of knowledge in this area or spend many hours analyzing or thinking about it. One of the oldest and biggest myths about investing is that most good investors spend hours and hours looking at charts and analyzing statistics when the truth is that it does not take that many hours to be able to do it. You simply need to acquire certain necessary habits and learn a little about the various financial assets that surround you without your awareness. It is normal that anyone reading this book wants to obtain a future of financial freedom, where they never have to worry about money again in their lives. What happens is that many people believe that this is impossible or consider that the only way to increase their lifestyle is to obtain a salary increase, when the truth is, many times, that ends up being a problem, not a solution. It seems crazy to say that a salary increase can become a problem, but it is the reality. When people receive a salary increase, they will generally not only have to pay more taxes but will also likely increase their level of debt. Since they will probably want to eat in more expensive restaurants, buy more expensive clothes, go out and have fun more often—all of which leaves them in the same financial position they were in before, or even worse.

This is because people often do not have a money problem but have problems with money management habits that do not allow them to manage their money intelligently. In order to do that, the first thing you have to understand is that there are three types of income (which you will see in much more detail throughout the book): earned income, passive income, and capital gains income. Of all these, the income that pays the most taxes is the earned income you receive in exchange for your work and is usually paid biweekly or monthly. Instead, in this book, we will focus on the various ways you can increase your passive income and build multiple sources of income, which will lead you to financial freedom in the future. Many people believe that financial freedom is about having a specific amount of money or something similar, but the truth is that this is a status that is all about freedom. This statement refers to the fact that financially free people can do what they want with their time since they do not need to go to work every day or receive orders from a boss all day.

Contrary to what many believe, financial freedom is obtained when you can pay all your expenses with your passive income. Passive incomes are those that are obtained without the need to work and are acquired, in general, through investments. That is why having a certain amount of money will not solve your problems, but you need to increase your passive income so that it can pay each of your monthly expenses and enable you to live peacefully without the need to work.

This book is divided into four parts so that you can learn the fundamentals related to the world of investments, regardless of your level of previous experience in each of these areas. In the first part, we will talk about how you can become a true investor. For example, many people believe that just buying stocks in some well-known companies like Facebook, Amazon, or Tesla will make them excellent investors and make them millionaires overnight. However, these things do not go hand in hand with investing, as they are pure speculation. Instead, being a true investor is about setting short- and long-term financial goals, developing an investment mind, and knowing how to manage your portfolio and money. It is also about building your emergency fund, knowing which are the ideal investments for you, and all of the basic things every investor needs to know. This will allow you to correctly introduce yourself to the world of investments, even if you have no previous experience in this area. In the second part of the book, we will talk about slightly more advanced things, such as how to start investing and what types of financial assets exist. We will also examine in detail many of the terms related to finances or investments that you may see in the news or on social media daily but don't know what they mean.

Later, in part three, you will learn the various low-risk investment mechanisms that you can use to multiply your savings and diversify your portfolio with long-term goals. One of the most important things you must know as a future investor is always trying to minimize risks. You must remember that when you invest, you are putting your money to work, but if you do not take into account the possible risks involved and all the things that can go wrong, then you can end up losing all that money and being left with nothing —and that is something that no one wants. That is why part three of the book will also be essential for you to start building your investment portfolio as a true expert and take into account the importance of continually reducing risks and understanding the symmetry that these have with the possible returns generated by an investment in the future. Finally, in part four of the book, you will learn the importance of not putting all your eggs in one basket. In other words, in this section, you will learn everything you need to know about diversifying your portfolio efficiently and effectively so that you can establish investment strategies that adapt to your needs and your long-term financial objectives.

Undoubtedly, one of the greatest desires people have is to achieve financial freedom so that they never have to work again and do not have to depend on work hours and a paycheck. That is why investments are increasingly important, as are terms such as compounding, which will define the final amount of money a person has obtained thanks to all their investments. That is why it is essential you start investing your money as soon as possible to take advantage of all the positive effects of compounding and reach your retirement age with the peace of mind that you have correctly planned your financial future. What do you say? Are you ready to start on this beautiful investing adventure and develop yourself as an incredible investor? If your answer was yes (and I am sure it was), then I do not doubt that you will become an excellent investor and that you will be able to achieve all your financial goals with the help of the knowledge obtained through reading this book.

1

KNOWING YOUR WHY

In part one of the book, we will focus mainly on developing a long-term investor mindset and understanding some of the fundamental concepts of finance and the world of investments that will lead you directly to success. One of the first things you should know before starting on this investment path is why you invest. People do not always invest for the same reasons: some people want to save for when the time comes to retire, others want to become rich overnight, others want to take advantage of certain tax advantages offered by investments, and others want to earn extra income, and of course, others want to achieve financial freedom. Therefore, the first thing you must do is define your objectives through investments, since in this way, you will know which are the most suitable for you and which are the most-recommended investment mechanisms. The problem with many people is that they start investing without a clear objective, which is never a good sign. Beginning to invest without a clear purpose is like starting to sail on the high seas without a compass or some direction in which you want to go. That is why you must know your why before making any move as an investor. There are many reasons why you should start investing, but these reasons may differ for each person; you must understand that what is suitable for some may be bad for others in the world of investments.

Throughout the book, you will learn a series of strategies that will help you make your own investment decisions, unlike many people who get carried away by the information they see on social networks. Or what some famous entrepreneurs or investors say. For example, some people only invest in well-known companies because they believe that these companies will never go bankrupt and that, therefore, they will be able to obtain a lot of profits. However, it is essential to know that just because a company is well-known does not mean it is a good investment for you. There are many cases of companies that are widely popular and have clients from all over the world that are unsuitable investments. It is likely that your favourite brand or company may not be a good investment for you since you must first do an analysis that allows you to know certain financial aspects of that company to determine if it is an excellent long-term investment. In the same way, you need to know that there is a series of habits you will need to acquire if you want to begin to be successful in the world of investments and multiply your money in the long term. All these aspects are questions that we will be looking at during the first part of this book since they are the essential foundation that will allow you to understand and apply the methodologies taught in the various chapters of this book.

WHY SHOULD YOU INVEST?

Without a doubt, investing your money is one of the most important things you must do in your life if you want to plan a financial future where money is not a problem. However, many people still do not understand the great importance of investments in their lives, which is why, in this section, we will review some of the most important points about why you should always invest your money. One of the essential things you need to know is that if you want to improve your financial situation, investments are your only solution. In other words, if you want to become a millionaire, have more income sources, elevate your lifestyle, or have more free time and not depend on a job. Therefore, you need to build sources of passive income that allow you to live calmly and without the need to work. The problem is that many people think that financial freedom is achieved by obtaining higher salaries, but as noted before, that ends up being a problem and not a solution.

There are many ways in which you can invest your money; fortunately, each of them can be easily adapted to your objective as a long-term investor. Another reason you should always invest your money is inflation. Inflation is the monetary phenomenon that causes the prices of goods or services in a country to rise generally and causes people's purchasing power to decrease more and more. Inflation has many causes, which are not relevant to this book's topic, but you need to know that this economic phenomenon can affect any country in the world. In fact, throughout history, the United States has been characterized as one of the countries with the most stable and robust economies in the world. Today, we can see how high inflation rates affect the entire population. However, people who invest their money intelligently suffer much fewer consequences due to inflation since compounding allows their money to multiply over time. Thus their profit margin is higher than the percentage of inflation in their country of residence. When we talk about compounding, we are referring to the process by which money multiplies exponentially over time, which is why throughout the book (and especially in the next chapter) you

will learn about the importance of time when we talk about investing successfully and having higher profits.

Another reason you should start investing is that money saved in the bank is devalued faster and faster. Of course, saving is one of the primary aspects that every investor must understand because if you do not save a certain part of your income, you simply will not have enough money to invest. It is not enough to keep your money in the bank, and that's it.

It would be best if you put it to work for you. Historically, the money saved in banks produces very little profit, in many cases none, since banks tend to offer a very low-interest rate on savings. Instead, inflation grows every day, making savings or parked money worth less and less. This is one of the most important reasons you should start investing as soon as possible. If your money always stays in a bank, then you will see how your purchasing power decreases every day. On the other hand, there are many wonderful things that you can achieve when you invest, since your money can multiply, and that would make your purchasing power increase every day.

RISKS OF NOT INVESTING

You have already seen some of the many reasons why you should start investing, but now you will also see some of the risks involved in not investing or simply not investing at the right time. One of those risks (and probably the one that most people worry about) is not having enough money when you reach retirement age. People usually work all their lives, arrive at work early, obey the orders of some boss, and at the end of the week or month, they receive a check with remuneration for all the hours they worked. However, many of these people believe that it is okay to live check-by-check and simply not save or invest anything. The truth is that this can be very dangerous because there will come a time when they don't want to or can't work anymore, and that means they need to have investments that give them passive income every month. Another risk that people who do not invest take is that it is very likely they will not be able to meet their financial goals in the short and long term. Everybody has specific goals or certain things they want to achieve in life, and one of them, without a doubt, is always to gain a better economic position than the one they have today.

That is why not investing can mean never improving your economic position. Finally, as noted earlier, people who don't invest may see their savings shrink due to inflation, low-interest rates offered by banks, or many other things that can affect their purchasing power. Similarly, people who do not invest are unprotected against possible events or unexpected situations that may occur and cause severe economic crises. For example, in the year 2020, when the COVID-19 pandemic began, many people sadly lost their jobs and saw their life savings disappear. That year was tough financially for the vast majority of people, especially for those who did not have any investment. However, many other people were protected from this type of situation since they had the help of investments that gave them passive income, so they did not depend only on a job or the current economic situation in their countries. Of course, that is not to say that investments are the solution to everything and do not involve risks or flaws, but certainly, investing will always be better than not investing for all the reasons that have been discussed.

THE BEST TIME TO INVEST

Many people and even professional investors try to make evaluations or statistical calculations to know when the best time is to enter a market or start investing. However, it is almost impossible to know this since people cannot accurately predict the market, not even economists and financial experts, so we cannot pretend to want to know the exact moment. In fact, most great investors who have managed to amass a huge fortune through investments usually say that it is much better to time yourself in the market than to try to time the market since the latter is something impossible. This means that, contrary to what many say, you should not try to wait for the perfect moment to invest since that moment may never come, and then you miss out on many good opportunities that may come your way. Instead, you should focus on being as consistent as possible, investing even a small amount of money every month, every week, every semester, or year. Still, you must maintain good discipline if you want to achieve something good with your investments. Undisciplined investors are doomed to failure, as they are often driven by emotions and want to become millionaires overnight when the truth is that this is impossible. That is why your approach must be to start investing as soon as possible and try to do it in the most intelligent way. In the future, you will see that this will bring you many economic benefits and peace of mind, which is the most important thing and the real reason for investing.

BETTER LATE THAN NEVER

People who start investing at an early age have many advantages since it is much easier to take advantage of compound interest's benefits (the evolution of how money has the power to multiply itself exponentially) that way. In other words, you have to do everything possible to start investing as soon as possible because if you leave this for later, you may be missing out on many opportunities offered by the world of investing. However, there are many people who, for various reasons, did not start investing early but instead have to do so when they are older. If this is your case, do not worry since you will still be able to take advantage of all the benefits of the world of investments, and you may even have some advantages. One of these advantages is that, in general, people who start investing at a later age tend to have greater financial security since they have savings that they have accumulated throughout their lives. Therefore, they can invest more money than those people who have not had as much savings throughout their careers.

Similarly, older investors are less likely to make impulsive or impatient decisions than investors who are newer to the world of investing. Of course, starting your trading career as early as possible is always better, but if you start a little late, it is not impossible to achieve good results. On the contrary, in the world of investments, there will always be opportunities for everyone; however, many people do not know how to take advantage of these opportunities.

SHORT TERM VS LONG TERM

One of the first things you should know as an investor is that there is a huge difference between investing for the short term and investing for the long term. The main difference is that when you invest for the short term, the market is much more volatile; therefore, your investments will have much higher risks. In contrast, when you invest for the long term, the market may or may not be volatile at the moment, but it will always correct itself in the future. Similarly, long-term investments are more beneficial since they will allow you to take advantage of each of the benefits of compound interest, so your money will be able to multiply exponentially and much more quickly. It is proven that people who invest with long-term goals have more advantages since it is more likely that they can earn money over time because the returns accumulate, and portfolios increase in value. Short-term investments are often described as speculative investments, such as the purchase of cryptocurrencies, for example, since they are investments that aim to multiply money quickly and easily. In general, short-term investments do not require as many analyses or complex methodologies to evaluate them. But are made by buying an asset and then selling it when the price increases. That is why the vast majority of experienced investors say that doing this type of thing is more like gambling in a casino than a real investment.

On the other hand, when we talk about long-term investments, they are those investments that do not have immediate liquidity. They do not turn into money in less than a year. Within this type of investment, you can include the purchase of shares in companies listed on the stock market, real estate, investments that provide dividends, or anything else designed to produce passive income for you over the long term. In general, expert investors recommend that it is better to make long-term investments than short-term ones since, as you will see below, they have many more advantages. Short-term investments have the benefit of allowing you to take advantage of the short volatility of the market and therefore be able to multiply your money quickly. However, they have the disadvantage that they tend to be much riskier, and investors should always try to reduce risks as much as possible. Similarly, short-term investments have the weakness of making people pay more taxes since they are considered earned income or capital gains income, unlike long-term investments that produce passive income with many more advantages. Short-term investments also tend to involve many of our emotions or instincts that lead us to make the wrong decisions when investing since, as you will learn in the second chapter, it is never good to involve your emotions in the world of investments.

On the other hand, although long-term investments do not have as much liquidity as short-term investments, they are characterized by the fact that they offer many tax advantages, just as they will allow you to benefit from all the advantages of compounding. People often underestimate the incredible power of compound interest, but the truth is that it is one of the most important factors when it comes to investing intelligently. If you invest your money in the short term, you will not be able to count on this beautiful advantage. Of course, there will always be financial advisors and accountants who will tell you that it is better to invest in the short term, but, in reality, the paths that lead to financial freedom are those of long-term investments. Accordingly, in this book, we will focus primarily on all those long-term investments that will help you multiply your money in an excellent way so that you can plan your financial future and make the best decisions regarding your money. In fact, if you look at some of the greatest investors in history, such as Benjamin Graham, Warren Buffett, Ray Dalio, Peter Lynch, Carl Icahn, and many others, you'll find that many of them are against short-term investments (except on certain occasions) because they all made their fortunes by investing intelligently and not by speculating since, in the world of investments, speculation is never reasonable.

Young investors may never have heard of Benjamin Graham, who was one of the greatest investors in history. That is why you are going to learn a little about his story, and we will talk about his investment philosophy so that you can take some advice directly from the most efficient investors in history. Benjamin Graham was one of the best investors of the 20th century and the teacher of one of the best investors of the 21st century: the great Warren Buffett. A lot of people don't know this, but Graham was Buffett's teacher when he attended one of his seminars; impressed by Graham's investment methodology, Buffet wanted to learn as much as possible about it. Graham is commonly known as the father of fundamental analysis, a type of analysis that investors do when deciding which companies to invest in. It requires them to look at certain aspects, such as the company's financial statements, the products it sells, the company's customer base, the news that revolves around it, the analysis of the competitors, and many other things that you will see throughout this book. The point is that one of the things that Graham emphasized the most, and that has helped many people become millionaires, is that time is vital in investments. This is why you should always try to invest for long terms; otherwise, you will be speculating and betting on the market, which is never a good thing since you should not put your money at risk.

Warren Buffett, for his part, learned as much as possible from Benjamin Graham and, little by little became interested in studying the fundamental analysis part of each of the companies he wanted to invest in. As a result, over the years, Buffett gained a great deal of experience and an excellent reputation in the market, which led him to found Berkshire Hathaway, one of the best-known and most successful investment funds in the world. Today, Buffett is one of the greatest investors in history and, indeed, one of the wealthiest men in the world. However, many people do not know that this man made most of his fortune after the age of 40, something that certainly does not happen every day. That is to say, during his first years as an investor, Buffett had to be very patient and disciplined when it came to investing. For he understood that this was the only way to be able to achieve great things in the market; otherwise, he would be another investor who failed in this process.

Contrary to what many people think, Buffett did not inherit his fortune or have a privileged childhood, although he had excellent training in the world of investments. Instead, he started out like many of us, since at first, he did not know anything about money or how the world economy moves, and today, even the presidents of the wealthiest countries ask him for advice on investing. This serves to make you realize that you can also achieve this type of success; it only requires a little discipline, perseverance and, of course, the necessary knowledge and patience to achieve it.

Segue: The Motivation to start investing should translate to action, so in the next chapter you will learn how to develop the mindset and habits of an investor.

2

DEVELOPING AN INVESTOR'S MINDSET AND HABITS

To be an excellent investor, you must not only have knowledge in the areas of economics, finance, and essential investment, but it is also vital that you develop the appropriate mindset and perspectives of most of the great investors at the international level. Many people think that to be a good investor, you only need a smartphone and money in your pockets, but the truth is that developing a good mindset for investments is necessary to allow you to achieve your long-term goals. Unfortunately, this is one area in which many people fail since sometimes they cannot develop this mindset but want to start investing only to multiply their savings. When we talk about a mindset, we describe the beliefs and convictions that a person has in their daily life. Of course, it is very difficult for two people to have the same mindset since this is part of our personality, which is unique. Therefore, it is likely that for you to become an excellent investor, you must leave behind some thoughts, beliefs, or convictions before you start investing. Because if you want to be successful in managing your money, you will have to change your way of thinking. For example, most people believe that they have money problems, that they do not have a big enough salary, or that they are not privileged enough to have inherited a fortune when most of the time, the real problem is in the way those people think.

When we say that the main problem is in the way people think and not in the amount of money they have saved in the bank, it is that people often do not know how to manage that money. Because they are accustomed to spending more than they have or believe they need to live for things that are simply unnecessary. For example, a person who has a salary of $2,000 a month, but does not know how to manage it, is likely to have many financial problems, be in debt, or simply have to work several jobs to survive. However, if a person who has a salary of $20,000 a month does not know how to manage it, then it is also possible that person has financial problems, is full of debt, or simply cannot have the lifestyle they want. This usually happens because people have many toxic financial habits, which lead them to manage their money poorly and cause them to be stressed or not know what to do to improve their situation. If you want to start investing successfully, you first have to get rid of all those toxic habits you have with money so that you can acquire new habits that will help you manage each of your investments. Many people believe that investments are a game where everyone wins; the truth is that there are risks involved, so it would be dangerous to start investing without first having the right mindset.

THE INVESTOR'S MINDSET

In this section, you will learn how to develop an investor mindset that will help you achieve your short- and long-term financial goals. One of the first things to know is that you may need to let go of certain habits in the past. In other words, you likely have specific practices that are not helping you to have a stable relationship with money but, on the contrary, are affecting how you manage your money. Therefore, one of the first things you must do to acquire an investor mindset is make an action plan. Unfortunately, some people do not carry out any financial plan and believe everything will be solved by chance. Unfortunately, this option never ends up being a reality since the only way to be successful in the world of investments is by following a roadmap; otherwise, you will be a ship adrift.

In the same way, you need to create a desire to succeed, since otherwise, you will always face your decisions when it comes to investing negatively, or you will always seek to go for the option with fewer risks and, therefore, less profit. All investors know that it is impossible to always win, so you will have to get used to accepting defeat from time to time. There are investors who are emotionally depressed after suffering some monetary loss, but that is how investments work, and that is why you should not let a defeat mark the way for you. Instead, you must learn the lessons of those decisions so that you can become a better investor every day. Next, you are going to see some of the key points and habits that you must take into account when developing an investor's mindset.

THE IMPORTANCE OF SAVINGS

One of the most important things to know when shifting to an investor mindset is that savings are not optional; they are mandatory. There are many people who believe that saving is a good thing because it will allow them to buy more things or simply increase their purchasing power, but, in fact, savings are what will define your ability to invest successfully. If you spend all the money you receive as a salary, you will be unable to invest, as you will not have available funds to do so. On the other hand, if you learn to allocate a part of your savings to investments, you will be much smarter when managing your money. One of the first things to know about saving is that you should always build an emergency fund before you start investing. You may have heard this term before, which means having a reserve of money (cash) that you can use in an emergency or a sudden situation requiring you to cover some unexpected expenses. We are all human; therefore, we can all catch a disease, have an accident, encounter certain unforeseen events that have to do with our vehicle, an international emergency, or simply anything else that requires money. With the emergency fund, you are guaranteeing that you are not going to touch the money that you have already invested, but rather that you will be able to cover each one of those emergencies quickly.

It is generally recommended that people build an emergency fund capable of covering at least three months of their fixed expenses before they start investing. If you do this, you will probably have to put a large percentage of your income into the emergency fund (for a few weeks or months), but it will be well worth it since, after that, you will be totally ready to invest. Many people believe this is unnecessary, but it is enough to go to 2020 to see the importance of emergency funds. In 2020, COVID-19 took the whole world by storm, and many people lost their jobs or were simply left in a pretty challenging financial situation. People who had a substantial emergency fund had a greater margin of time to plan what they were going to do to solve those economic problems; unfortunately, those who did not have money saved simply could not enjoy those benefits and found themselves in a difficult financial situation. Of course, nobody wants these things to happen again. Still, it would help if you were prepared so that when an unexpected problem arises, you have an emergency fund to protect yourself. Similarly, savings are super significant because they will allow you to start investing continuously, which is one of the keys to success in the world of investments. Later, when we talk about budgets, you will learn much more about efficient ways to save money for investment purposes.

Credit Cards

Around the world, credit cards are one of the most-used financial instruments by people on a daily basis. This is because the credit system allows people to buy things they cannot afford since it allows them to spend money they do not have. Almost nobody tells us that the financial world works through debt, which is why banks issue so many credit cards with very high consumption limits; in this way, people can spend a lot, and then they have to pay a lot of money later in interest. Having a credit card is necessary, and it's not bad. The bad thing is how many people use it since they believe it is a source of infinite money; they do not realize or accept that this type of consumption can have severe consequences in the future, both in the short term and in the long term. The vast majority of banks charge high interest for transactions made through credit cards. Many people make the mistake of simply making the minimum payment on those cards in order to continue borrowing and accumulating more purchases through those cards, which is a grave mistake. It would be best if you always tried to accumulate as little debt as possible; what credit cards do most of the time is encourage unnecessary debt, as many people don't know how to use them.

However, despite what many people think, debt is not always bad, although this might seem absurd. For this, you must remember that the financial status of each person is divided into two large columns, which are assets and liabilities. Within the asset's column, you have all those things that are capable of putting money in your pockets, such as stocks, bonds, certificates of deposits, cash, real estate, vehicles, businesses, patents, products that can be sold, and many other things that you can turn to. On the other hand, within the liability's column, there will be all those things that take money out of your pocket in one way or another, such as credit card debt, mortgages, bank loans, student loans, subscriptions, and many other things that you have to pay regularly. Of course, if you go into debt to go out to dinner with your friends, buy tickets to a concert, or buy a new car, you are pretty likely resorting to bad debt. However, if you ask for a loan to buy a real estate property and put it up for rent, in which the payment that the tenant gives you is greater than the amount of the bank loan that you have to pay every month, then it is a good debt. Since you are acquiring an asset greater than the liability, it will put money in your pocket. Of course, as you begin your career as an investor, it would be best if you had as little debt as possible.

Budgeting

The budget is another thing that should never be missing during your financial planning, much less during this new path as an investor. Many believe that a budget is simply dividing the money for the things they have to pay. Still, it goes much further than that because budgeting involves the correct financial planning necessary to succeed in investing. In general, people who tend to spend money impulsively or simply do not manage their money correctly are those who do not have a budget. This is very serious because if you do not have a budget, you are much more likely to make mistakes with your money and want to spend more than you have.

On the other hand, a budget sets the limits between what you have and what you can spend and allows you to save, invest, and pay all your expenses in a much more orderly way. Of course, budgets are individual since each person has different expenses, needs, tastes, and incomes. However, certain standardized methodologies can help you when making your budget. Best of all, they are methodologies and strategies that have been proven by financial experts for a long time, so you can fully trust them.

One of those budgeting strategies that you can use is the 70/30 rule. This proposes that with 70% of your monthly income, pay all your debts and expenses, and with the remaining 30% of that income, divide it in half, save part, and invest another part. That is, in the end, 70% of your income will be for essential things, such as food, rent, car insurance, your children's clothes, gasoline, and all those fixed and variable expenses that you have to pay every month. 15% will go to your emergency fund, and the remaining 15% can be used to invest. However, many times people complain that this budgeting system does not consider that people also need a little money for entertainment and leisure. That is why the 50/30/20 strategy also arises, which states that 50% of your income will cover your variable and fixed expenses, 30% will be for entertainment, and the remaining 20% will be divided between savings for the emergency fund and investments. In this way, if you earn $1,000 a month, $500 will be for your fixed expenses, $300 will be for things like going to the movies, going out to eat with friends or other forms of entertainment, and $100 will be to save in your emergency fund. The remaining $100 will be invested in any of the investment mechanisms you will discover throughout this book. You can use any strategy you want, always remembering that budgeting must be flexible because if you do not, you will become bored, and you will want to abandon that budgeting method.

Pay Yourself First

One of the things that you must do when you become an investor, but that, unfortunately, very few people do, is to pay yourself first. This may seem a bit confusing, but it is the key that will lead you to having more money to invest. What most people do when they receive their salary is pay taxes (if they have not already been deducted automatically), pay mortgage payments, pay debts, loans, gas, insurance, and all the other fixed expenses. And then they buy some clothes or spend money on many things they don't need. Worst of all is that those people leave saving cash to the last, and then they make the excuse that they simply had nothing left to save.

The truth is that the problem is not that they don't have enough money to save but that they have already spent it all on things that weren't necessary or urgent. So, what you must prioritize before making purchases for leisure or entertainment is to pay yourself first, since that is how you make sure that you will have money to invest, save, or simply move to your emergency fund. Do not pay everyone first through payments that are not always necessary, but prioritize paying yourself first; that way, you'll always have money to save and invest.

INCREASING YOUR INCOME

Most people spend their time looking for different ways to increase their income, but what many do is only lower their expenses. Of course, it is also vital that you lower your expenses a little, especially those that are unnecessary. But what is truly important is that you can increase your income sources through investments and the passive income that each of those investments will generate for you. There are many ways to improve your revenue. However, if it is through investments, it will be much better since, as we have said repeatedly, when people have an increase in their salary, they generally tend to increase their debts and expenses. Despite what many believe, increasing your sources of passive income through investments is effortless, and it takes little time to do so. The vast majority of people tend to think that to invest successfully, you have to spend an hour glued to the television or analyzing graphs and statistics, but, in reality, investment valuation methods are much simpler than that. In this book, you will find effective and realistic ways to increase your income level in a simple way that will help you increase your purchasing power.

Segue: You've been bolstering your motivation and enhancing your financial outlook and habits. Only one more component remains for you to obtain so you can start investing successfully, and that is a thorough understanding of the different investment options available to you. You'll get into this in the next chapter.

3

MASTERING ASSET CLASSES AND INVESTMENT OPTIONS

One of the most important things when you are investing, is that you have to understand the financial assets in which you are putting your money. There are many people who have the desire to start investing, but simply do not know how to do it since they do not understand some financial assets such as stocks, bonds, or cryptocurrencies or they just do not know how the market works. Nevertheless, many of these people still risk investing their money in things they don't know about, and often end up losing that money because they didn't know how to manage those investments. Do not make that mistake; make sure you understand the financial assets in which you are investing, as well as the level of risk that each of them involves and the possible returns that they will generate. In this way, you will be able to keep an eye on the returns that these investments generate, the ideal time to exit an investment, when to reinvest, and all the other aspects that you should know when entering this wonderful world of investments and personal finance. Of course, there are many people who know exactly what they are investing in, and still end up losing money or making poor decisions, as the market is a volatile system that can change overnight and is totally unpredictable.

UNDERSTANDING ASSET MIX

One of the first things you should understand about the world of investments is that in a portfolio, you must have multiple investments, which is commonly called diversification. That is, you should never put all your eggs in one basket since, in this way, you will depend on a single sector, a single company, or a single investment. On the other hand, people who diversify their portfolios are much more protected against a possible catastrophe to a company or a specific sector in which they have invested. In fact, most of the expert investors and millionaires in the world understand that diversification is one of the fundamental keys to being successful in investing, and they, themselves, have well-diversified investment portfolios. However, there are many people who do not understand this concept precisely and believe that diversification is simply investing in some low-risk investment mechanism that is not as volatile. For example, many people believe that investing in a mutual fund is being diversified since it is something that has low risk and is managed by experts. However, this is the opposite of being diversified since you are putting all your money into one thing. Even worse, you are leaving it in the hands of so-called experts who might only be interested in the commissions they earn. Therefore, it's essential to really learn the meaning of asset mix and how you can use it in each of your investments quickly and easily.

Here is a simple example that will help you understand what an asset mix is all about. Suppose you have $1,000 available to invest, and you want to invest all of it by buying Tesla stocks, as it is a well-known company and has generated good returns in recent years. Many people do this and believe they are investing the right way. However, this is wrong and could lead to ruin since you will be depending only on one company, and if that company were to fail one day for any reason, you would lose your money. Instead, it would be much wiser to divide that money into multiple parts and put each of those parts into different investments. For example, divide that $1,000 into several parts: $200 in stocks, $200 in bonds, $200 in an index fund, $200 in a real estate investment trust, and the other $200 in a certificate of deposit. That is proper diversification since you are not depending on only one industry or one company; instead, you will have a varied investment portfolio that is going to contain many investments. Some of which are safer, and others that have a slightly higher level of risk; this is perfect since you will have a balanced investment portfolio, which is what every investor wants to achieve. Of course, some people also decide to put 100% of their money in a single item, such as $1,000 in stocks or bonds. This is also a strategy that can pay off, but only if you also diversify. That is, in this case, you could invest $200 in Facebook stocks, $200 in Tesla stocks, $200 in Coca-Cola, $200 in Carnival, and $200 in Apple. In this way, you will have a portfolio of stocks, but one that does not depend on a single company or a single business sector.

A QUICK GUIDE TO STOCKS FOR BEGINNER INVESTORS

In the previous section, you learned that there is a way to diversify and invest through stocks. This is probably one of the most popular forms of investment today and has been so throughout history. However, there are many people who do not know how stocks work or who simply do not know some of the basic characteristics that these stocks have and the correct ways in which to invest. In this section, you will learn everything related to stocks in a simple way so that you can know what they are, how they work, and how you can start investing in these financial assets and take advantage of all their benefits. This way, you will be able to ensure that you know what you are doing and invest your money correctly. Unfortunately, there are many people who invest in a particular stock just because they are well-known or because they have seen them on television. That was what happened with Tesla; at the beginning, people wanted to buy stocks under the premise that they were going to make a lot of money quickly and easily, but you should know that stocks are not a game. They are serious investments that should be taken as such; otherwise, you can end up losing a lot of money. Don't worry; this stock guide will be as understandable as possible so that you can learn each of the factors that surround these financial assets, which are probably the favorites of most investors.

When we talk about stocks, we are referring to a portion of a company that is listed on the stock market and can be bought by any investor around the world. That is, when you buy a stock in a company, you are acquiring a tiny portion of that company, which is undoubtedly something very beneficial for all investors since it allows them to take advantage of all the benefits and returns generated by that company. The stocks are issued through something known as the Initial Public Offering (IPO), which we will explain with this simple example. Suppose Peter has a small business in Chicago that makes shoes. As that company is small, Peter only manages to sell the shoes to people who are close to him, friends, and family; but little by little, the business expands as the popularity of these shoes grows. Eventually, Peter sees that his business is growing very strongly, and he decides to create another branch of the company in Miami and another in

New York. Peter's business continues to be a success in those three cities, with increasing annual profits and increased sales. However, Peter wants to expand nationally and wants to have a store in every state in the country. For that, he needs a lot of capital, so he decides that the time is right for his company to go public.

During the IPO, the company issues 100,000 shares (stocks), available to all those investors who want to participate. The price of these stocks will be determined by the level of supply and demand they have on any given day. Suppose that the initial price of those stocks is $10, from which the company will be able to raise $1,000,000 in order to continue expanding and make other investments; each person who bought those stocks becomes a shareholder of the company. Each of those people will be able to sell those stocks later to other investors, and the price of those stocks will continue to be determined by the laws of supply and demand. In economics, when a product or service has a much higher demand than the supply, the price tends to increase, and when the supply is much higher than the demand, the price tends to decrease. The same thing happens with the traditional stock market, except companies issue millions of stocks, and there are millions of investors eagerly waiting to buy those companies' stocks. After those investors become shareholders, there are two basic ways to make money. The first is through capital gains. That is, suppose a month ago you bought stock in a company for $100, and today you sell it at a price of $125; that leaves you with a profit of $25. The second way you can make money with stocks is through passive income. For that, you have to invest in those companies that have a dividend policy, which will be explained later in this section.

The stocks are traded through stock exchanges and other exchanges. The two most prominent in the world (and in history) are the New York Stock Exchange (NYSE) and the national association of securities dealers automated quotations (NASDAQ). The NYSE was established a few centuries ago on Wall Street, but it worked in a much more rudimentary way than it does now. For its part, NASDAQ was created in 1971, so it is relatively new. Nevertheless, the way both works is very similar; companies with a long history in the stock market, such as Ford, Coca-Cola, or Walmart, are usually listed on the NYSE.

On the other hand, in NASDAQ, you find companies that are a little newer and that are more likely to be related to technology, such as Tesla, Apple, Facebook, or Microsoft. There are many indicators and indices that are used to help you know the current market situation just by looking at indices like the Standard and Poor's 500 (S&P 500) and the Dow Jones Industrial Average (DJIA). These are stock indices that basically take all prices of stocks of the companies that are listed on the various stock exchanges and turn them into a single number so that the market situation can be analyzed more easily and more quickly. The S&P 500 takes the top 500 companies listed on the stock market, while the DJIA is much more exclusive as it only takes the 30 most valuable companies on the stock market. In other words, these indices are used so that you can see how the stock market is doing based on the most important and solid companies in the market; these are the ones that usually set the course for the stock market.

How Can You Invest in Stocks?

It is likely that after reading all the information regarding stocks, you are wondering how you can start investing in them, and the answer is straightforward: through an online broker. Many people believe that the world of investments is reserved for expert economists or that only prominent business people can buy stocks in big companies, but the truth is that anyone can. In fact, today, the only thing you need in order to invest in a smartphone and Wi-Fi, besides money, of course. Previously, when the Internet was not as developed, investing was a bit more complex, where people had to go to the bank, meet with the bank's financial or investment advisor, and then make the investment or purchase of stocks. As if that were not enough, the investor also had to pay hefty commissions, which ended up negatively impacting the investor's profits.

Moreover, those commissions that you paid did not assure you any profit since these advisors, or individual brokers charged you once they made the investment, regardless of the final result. So today, you have the enormous benefit of using the Internet for investing; since many online brokers do not charge a commission, you can invest without paying a large commission. That is why we can say that all these new online investment platforms have served to democratize and further expand the world of finance since each person can access large investments without any problem.

To open an account with an online broker, you only need some personal identification, such as a passport, driver's license, or something similar, and your bank details—that's it; after that, you can start investing in stocks. Of course, depending on the country where you live, you will have a certain number of online brokers available. Each of them will have certain advantages and disadvantages that will help you determine which one is best for you. One of the most well-known online brokers today is Robinhood, which is a platform where you can invest quickly, safely, easily, and best of all, without commissions. However, at the moment, this platform is only available to residents of the United States. There are other platforms such as TD Ameritrade, Acorns, and Stash that offer the same service as Robinhood. They have the advantage that they are also available to residents of many other countries, so you can take advantage of this enormous opportunity and start buying stocks from the comfort of your home. Of course, you must remember that this is not a game; because of the ease that exists today to buy stocks, many people have started to invest a lot of money without having a clear investment strategy. Instead, they purchase popular stocks or other financial assets without really knowing why they are investing. The good thing is that through this book, you will learn to develop the basic habits that every investor should have; you will also acquire specific knowledge that will help you analyze and determine the best investments for you and the best companies in which you can invest.

Benefits of Owning Stock

Investing in stocks has many benefits, especially when you have a long-term investment perspective. One of the primary benefits of owning stock is that you will be part-owner of the company and, therefore, you will be able to take advantage of many of the benefits and returns that the company generates. Of course, it does not mean that if you buy a stock in Apple, you will be a full owner since we know that this is one of the most valuable companies in the world, and it would be absurd to think that we can buy it with $200 or $300. However, when you are a shareholder in Apple, you will be able to enjoy some of the benefits that owners have; for example, you will benefit when the price of that stock rises. In addition, when you buy stocks in a company that issues dividends, you will receive quarterly passive income. That happens simply because you hold that stock, and then that passive income can be reinvested in that same company or any other. That way, you can take advantage of the compounding interest that is generated in your portfolio so that you have an ever-increasing investment amount. Another reason to keep stocks in your portfolio is that they allow you to combat inflation. Fiat money (the one that is printed by the government), which is what you have right now in your pocket or in your bank account, is devalued since it does not generate dividends or passive income but instead loses more and more value thanks to inflation.

On the other hand, when a person owns some stock, it is possible that it not only generates passive income in the form of dividends but can also possibly generate a lot of profit in the long term because you could then sell it for a higher price. People who have stocks in their investment portfolios are already beginning to diversify because they are investing in one of the financial assets that have generated the highest returns throughout history and which have proven to be investments that, in the long term, usually generate profits. People who invest in stocks can not only invest in individual companies, but they can also invest in index funds and Exchange Traded Funds (ETFs). Index funds are investment funds that are guided by the returns of a specific index, such as the S&P 500 or the DJIA. The good thing about this type of investment is that you do not depend on a single company. Instead, you will have the security of having invested in many companies at the same time, which significantly reduces the risk of that investment and increases the chances of earning a profit. For their part, ETFs are stock bags or groups that are sold individually but enable you to invest in many companies in specific industries at the price of what stock of an individual company cost. These last two types of investment (stocks and ETFs) are excellent options since the market has shown over time that, in the long term, it usually has a return of at least eight per cent (except in years where there have been financial crises).

WHAT ABOUT BONDS?

Another of the better-known financial products in the market is bonds, both government and corporate. When we talk about a bond, we are referring to a loan that you make to a government institution or to a company in exchange for obtaining interest on that loan. In the end, the issuer will return the amount that you initially invested, and you will have earned some interest. In other words, this is the opposite of what happens when you are the one who asks for a loan from a bank, where not only do you have to repay all the money, but you will also have to pay a certain amount of interest on that loan. We must clarify that within the world of investments, investing in bonds is one of the safest ways that exists; however, since there are not so many risks involved, it is also one of the ways that give investors the least returns. Bonds usually have a rating, where AAA is the best rating a bond can get, which means that the risk of that bond defaulting (not getting your money back) is relatively low. However, the safer a bond is, the fewer rewards it will have. Generally, the safest bonds are government bonds since the Federal Reserve can't go bankrupt. However, corporate bonds are sometimes dangerous since these companies can default on payments if they have some financial problems that may affect the liquidity of that company.

Segue: Becoming a successful investor means learning how to identify and avoid or manage risk. It is a crucial skill you can't overlook and it's the topic of the next chapter.

4

UNDERSTANDING INVESTMENT RISKS

As we have mentioned several times throughout this book, there is no investment that is risk-free, as all investments, even the ones that seem very safe, have even a small percentage of risk. You have to be very careful where you invest when evaluating each of those risks and make sure that those risks are not going to affect your portfolio in the long term. The important thing is not that you look for an investment that does not have any risk since you are not going to be able to get that type of investment in the market; the important thing is that you know what risks investments have, and then you will know if you are willing to take those risks. Not all people have the same level of risk tolerance because there are some who seek to invest in other things that are safer, thereby generating fewer returns, while other people only seek to invest in things that generate high returns. Therefore, the first thing you should do is an internal evaluation of how much risk you are willing to assume; that way, when analyzing an investment, you will be able to see how compatible it is with your portfolio. Similarly, it should be noted that there are investment sectors that are much riskier than others. For example, investing in cryptocurrencies and investing in bonds do not have the same risk, since bonds are much safer, and it is almost impossible for them to go unpaid.

Cryptocurrencies are characterized as being totally volatile financial products, which can go up or down in price from one day to the next. This is often good because it means that you can make big profits in a short time, but other times it can be very bad since you can lose your money very quickly, which nobody wants. Apart from the risks involved in each of the investments individually, such as the two examples just mentioned, there are also certain intrinsic risks that do not have to do with the investments but, rather, with external factors that can directly affect your investments. We are going to define each of these factors in this chapter, so that you can easily identify them and develop a good investment plan to be prepared for them. That is why we are going to divide these types of intrinsic risks into two parts: systematic risks and unsystematic risks. In general, systematic risks are those that occur cyclically and, therefore, are impossible to avoid no matter what country you live in. On the other hand, unsystematic risks are those that can vary depending on the country, on politics, or on macroeconomic issues. The important thing is that each of these risks can have direct implications on your investment portfolio.

SYSTEMATIC RISKS

Inflation

One of the most common economic phenomena in history and today is inflation. In simple terms, inflation is the general increase in the prices of goods and services in a country and is measured in percentage terms. That is, when it is said that a country has an annual inflation rate of 15%, it means that there has been a yearly increase in the prices of most products and services by 15%. As expected, inflation is extremely bad as it decreases the purchasing power of people since, in general, countries with high inflation rates do not usually have companies that give salary increases that might mitigate the terrible effects of this situation. Most politicians say that inflation can be caused by many things, but the truth is that the main cause of inflation is the money supply. The monetary issue generates a fictitious increase in the aggregate financial demand of a country; as public spending increases, the country is forced to raise taxes. All this causes economic chaos that is reflected in inflation. What happens is that governments often (even if they don't say so) benefit from the monetary issue since, in this way, they can increase public spending. Inflation can be lethal for your investments if, for example, you invest in a financial product that generates returns of eight per cent per year. Still, the annual inflation is five per cent; you will only earn three per cent.

That is why you must always keep in mind the various risks of inflation. Of course, none of us can control inflation since that is something that the politicians or economic authorities of each of the countries should do. However, inflation usually ends up getting out of control and causing adverse effects such as those that are being seen today in many countries. There are financial assets that are more sensitive to inflation than others, and you should be very careful with that. For example, bonds, which are fixed-income financial assets, are the investments that suffer the most from inflation since the amount of your money, as well as the interest that you are going to receive, is fixed. When inflation increases, the money that this bond will generate will not increase.

On the other hand, in times of inflation, people who have their money invested in stocks have more advantages since stocks tend to appreciate in times of inflation, as they are not fixed-income assets, and their prices are volatile. That is why you should always take inflation into account when analyzing an investment, even if you think you live in a country with a lot of economic stability. For example, throughout history, the United States has always been one of the countries with the most stable economies, but at present, it is going through a painful period of inflation, from which no world economy is entirely safe.

Interest Rate Changes

Interest rates also play a fundamental role in any economy. This is because a change in interest rates, however small, means that all the ways in which people ask for money, as well as some financial assets such as bonds, will change radically. As you well know, when a person goes to a bank to request a loan, the bank makes it a condition that they will have to pay certain interest on a monthly, quarterly, every four months, or even on an annual basis (depending on the conditions of that loan). In the same way, when someone buys a certificate of deposit or simply invests in a government bond, that person is informed of the interest rate that the issuer will pay in exchange for their money and, accordingly, that person knows if that investment interests them or not. A small change in interest rates promulgated by the central bank of any country, the Federal Reserve, or any other monetary authority will radically change each of these investments or financial conditions of loans and bonds. That is why, despite the fact that many times people believe that interest rates are not so relevant, they end up being very important for your investments. In general, interest rates are only changed in extreme economic circumstances since they are usually increased at times when inflation is accelerating strongly and are often decreased when the country is in stable economic conditions since what is sought is that people begin to invest their money in other things, thereby generating a rise in aggregate demand and in the country's consumption.

UNSYSTEMATIC RISKS

Liquidity Risk

The liquidity that each investment has can also vary drastically depending on the financial asset you choose since there are some that can be converted into cash more quickly and easily than others. For example, cryptocurrencies and most stocks are financial assets with a lot of financial liquidity since the investor can decide to sell them at any time and will obtain the money almost immediately. However, suppose someone invests in bonds, certificates of deposit, or any other financial instruments. In that case, the liquidity is not so great since it will cost much more to sell them and for that money to be credited quickly. For this, you will have to evaluate the level of liquidity of each of the financial assets you will invest in to avoid any surprises later. The mistake that many people make is that they believe that they will be able to get out of those investments whenever they want, but the world of finance does not work like that; there are investments that simply do not have a high level of liquidity, and therefore, it is much more difficult to obtain the money you invest quickly and easily without losing out. On the other hand, when you know an investment's level of liquidity, it will be much easier to establish a term in which you will be able to recover or multiply your money.

Mismanagement Risk

This is probably one of the most common risks that you will find when investing, but it depends on your experience and your emotional intelligence since it refers to the ability you have to manage your portfolio in an organized manner. Unfortunately, many people simply get carried away by emotions or do not have the necessary skills or habits to manage an investment portfolio in an organized manner. However, this risk can be mitigated through experience, and of course, through all the knowledge that you will be able to acquire through this book.

Political Risk

This is a risk that will always be present in any country since there are very few countries that have total political stability; many countries tend to have political instabilities, and that generally causes people to lose confidence in the national economy, and multiple crises arise that can jeopardize your portfolio. However, this is a risk that will always be present in most countries. Unfortunately, you cannot do anything to change it other than be patient and hope that these problems do not become more significant than they already are.

INVESTMENT APPROACHES

There are many perspectives through which you can start making your investments, and of course, each of these will be based on the financial objectives that you have in the long term. But unfortunately, many people believe that there is only one way to invest or that it is simply about depositing money in their investment account and hoping that a miracle will happen. The truth is that this is very far from reality because the idea is to design an investment plan that contains your strategies and objectives in order to be clear about which are the most appropriate financial assets for you.

Growth Investing

In general, when talking about growth investing, experts refer to all those investments that aim to multiply your money exponentially in the long term. In general, this type of investment can bring enormous returns, but as expected, it also brings a fairly high level of risk. However, as you learned in the previous section, these risks can be mitigated. If you are going to invest with this approach, you must be careful not to bet that a company or a financial asset will be successful in the long term; you must really analyze the reasons why that investment will make your money grow. In the long term, growth investments often stop growing and become more stable investments, but you will have already made money by then. One of the clear examples of this type of investment is Amazon. During the beginning of this company, everyone was talking about how Amazon was going to change the business world completely, and therefore, when the company was listed on the stock market, many investors rushed to put their money in Amazon stocks. Without a doubt, this is one of the cases where a possible growth investment ended up being successful.

Unfortunately, this does not happen with all companies. For example, Zynga was one of the most coveted companies by investors around the year 2007 since it was one of the leading companies in the technology and video game sector. Everyone thought that this was going to be the next big company, especially because of the rapid growth it was having and the enormous popularity it had among technology fans. However, it all fell apart as the company grew too fast, and management didn't know how to manage all the sudden success. The company is still going strong today, but it's nowhere near becoming the company many investors hoped would be the next leader in the tech world. This is why you have to be careful when you carry out a growth investing strategy since companies do not always end up reaching their full potential.

Value Investing

Another of the approach that investors often give to investments is that of value investing. This is about knowing a company's intrinsic value and investing only if it is undervalued. That is to say, people who are dedicated to making value investments generally try to invest in companies that basically have a discount price. This is not so easy since you have to perform a fundamental analysis where you have to analyze and evaluate the financial statements of the company, the decisions of the board of directors, the level of sales, the level of participation in the market, and many other important financial statistics. This type of approach is often attributed to Benjamin Graham, who, as we said in the first chapter, is the father of value investing. Today, many world-renowned investors such as Warren Buffett and Charlie Munger are engaged in this type of investment, and it has generated billions of dollars for them. One of the most significant advantages of this type of investment is that investors have access to investments at a discount price, but it has the disadvantage that it does not always give huge returns.

Income Investing

Finally, there is the income investing strategy, which refers to all those investments that provide investors with passive income. In general, this type of investment is not designed to multiply your money exponentially in the long term but to provide you with a fixed income from time to time as interest, dividends, or any other type of passive income. An example of this may be investing in AT&T or Coca-Cola stocks, which pay dividends from time to time to their shareholders. Of course, these dividends might be no more than three per cent of the stock price at that time, but the idea is to accumulate and reinvest each of those dividends and thus make your passive income grow more and more.

Segue: At this point, you are now mentally prepared to start investing. Part 2, starting with the next chapter, covers the other main aspect, which consists of the practical considerations in investing.

5

CHOOSING THE RIGHT INVESTMENTS

During the first part of the book, the idea was that you would be acquiring more knowledge and everyday habits of great world investors.

In this second part, we will delve much more deeply into the world of investments, and you are going to discover different ways of analyzing some investments, selecting them and, of course, learning some rules and principles that you must take into account when putting your money in a possible investment.

CHOOSING INVESTMENTS AND PUTTING TOGETHER A PORTFOLIO THAT WORKS FOR YOU

One of the most important things you should know when starting to invest in the way in which you should build your portfolio. In this case, we are not referring to whether you are going to invest more money in stocks or bonds but in the things that you must take into account when choosing a possible investment. You should know that when you choose an investment, you are making a long-term commitment to yourself, similar to marriage because you are going to have to have a lot of trust in that investment, a lot of patience, and tolerance. You must know how to understand it, and of course, leave it in difficult times. This may seem a bit humorous, but it is a metaphor that is used a lot in the investment world. There are many investors who lack much-needed investing habits, such as patience or motivation; many times, that ends up costing them dearly in the long run, and they end up losing money.

Investing by Risk Tolerance

As we have said on multiple occasions, not all investments carry the same degree of risk, and not all people have the same level of risk tolerance. That is why, when you are evaluating an investment, you need to know the level of risk that it has. For example, a person who wants to invest safely because they do not have a high-risk tolerance should not invest in stocks of a new technology company since these types of growth investments have a high degree of risk. Instead, that person should invest in stocks of companies with a long history in the market that provides greater security, such as Coca-Cola, AT&T, Visa, or other similar companies.

Investing by Objective

The objectives you have in the world of investments should be the ones that guide each of your decisions. In other words, if your goal is to be able to start planning your financial future properly, and to have a good base of savings and passive income for when the time comes to retire, then you are going to invest in investment mechanisms that offer stability and long-term returns. On the other hand, if you want to start investing simply because you want to put your savings to work for you, then you can choose some fixed-income financial assets. That is to say, there are many objectives that you can have in the world of investments, and you must let those objectives be what help you make your decisions since otherwise, it will be similar to going on a ship adrift.

Investing by Time Horizon

Finally, it is always vital that you take into account the time frame in which you want your investments to develop. There are people who want to recover their money quickly, there are others who always want their investments to have enough liquidity, and there are others who do not care that they cannot touch that money for years since their goals are to invest for the long term. Without a doubt, the time horizon you have for your investments is going to be very important because if you analyze this factor well, then you won't have to worry about your investments or have any unexpected surprises since you will know perfectly when you are going to invest, recover your money, or at least when you will be able to reinvest it.

KEEP IN MIND THE 80/20 RULE

There is a fundamental principle within the world of finance and economics known as the Pareto Principle. What this says is that 80% of your income will come from 20% of your investments. That is to say, there is going to be a group of investments that are going to be the ones that generate the highest returns, but that is totally enough to achieve a good level of returns and thus multiply your money. Many times, people believe that they need to have many successful investments in order to earn money and, therefore, they want to have a very large portfolio since they consider that this is the only way to multiply their money. However, that is very far from reality. You do not need to have a huge investment portfolio, but you do need powerful investment accounts that generate the necessary returns so that you can enjoy the results of good long-term financial planning.

THE IMPORTANCE OF COMPOUNDING

In order to help you understand the importance of compounding in investments, we will review an example that can occur in everyday life. Suppose there are two friends who want to invest their money, one named John and the other named Eli. They are both 25 years old, but only John is willing to start investing since Eli prefers to spend that money on other things at the moment and gain more experience. John decides that he is going to invest $5,000, and he does that every year without interruption until he is 35 years old. After that, John decides that he is not going to invest anymore and that he is just going to let compounding take over, multiplying that $50,000 that he invested (it was $5,000 every year for ten years). At that moment, at age 35, Eli decides that now he will start investing, and he invests the same amount as John ($5,000) but for 30 years in a row. When they are 65 years old, they want to retire. Thanks to the effects of compounding, as incredible as it may seem, the one who achieved greater profits was John, who only invested $50,000, rather than Eli, who invested $150,000. Assuming they both earned fixed returns of 8 per cent per year, by age 65, John would have amassed a total of $787,000 and Eli a total of about $612,000. This is the enormous power that compounding has; unfortunately, even so, many people underestimate the benefits of starting to invest as soon as possible. Nobody will be 100% prepared to start investing, but you must dare to start making all those decisions that will, undoubtedly, have a positive impact on your future.

TYPES OF RISK PROFILE

Next, we will examine which investor profile you belong to based on your risk tolerance. Of course, none of these profiles is better than another, but they will help you discover which are the most suitable financial assets and investment mechanisms for you. People can change their profiles as time pass by since this is greatly influenced by the person's age, needs, long-term goals and, of course, the amount of money they are willing to invest.

It is not unusual that your profile might change.

Conservative

In general, conservative investors are those who do not prioritize high profits but accept profits and invest in financial assets that are pretty safe. In general, people who are already a little advanced in age or who simply already have a good savings base are usually conservative investors since they know that for them, the most important thing is to maintain economic stability and be able to increase their savings a little. This type of investor usually invests in issues such as treasury bills, corporate bonds, sovereign bonds, or simply in companies that have maintained a stable path in the stock market.

Moderate

Moderate investors are those who prioritize both profits and safety, so they invest in investment mechanisms that provide good profits but do not have a high level of risk. In other words, this type of investor wants to multiply their savings, but they also prefer to not take many risks by investing in things that are very volatile. In general, these types of investors are those people who have a stable job, who want to increase their savings base or their retirement fund, and also want to gradually achieve financial freedom. Therefore, the vast majority of these investors invest their money in index funds, income stocks, or any other investment mechanism that provides them with security but at the same time ensures that they obtain a good amount of income.

Aggressive

Finally, we have aggressive investors, who are those who are willing to take more risks in order to obtain much higher profits. Generally, these types of investors are young people who still have nothing to lose, so they can go further and take higher risks to try to obtain enormous profits. This type of investor usually invests in growth stocks, corporate bonds that are not as safe but offer a lot of returns, or simply in issues that are volatile and may not have as much liquidity since what they want is to increase their money significantly.

As you can see, there is no investor profile that is better than another. We have outlined some of the qualities and skills of these people, and these characteristics end up being key when making investment decisions.

Segue: In the next chapter, you'll learn how to effectively track your investments.

6

KEEPING TRACK OF YOUR INVESTMENTS

There is a very important saying that is used in finance that states that everything that can be measured can be improved. Similarly, management experts often say that if we don't measure something, we just can't tell if it's working or if we're getting the results, we wanted in the first place. When it comes to investing, you are going to have to manage your investments, and that means that you will have to develop certain skills that will allow you to control and measure each of your investments.

WHY YOU SHOULD KEEP TRACK OF YOUR INVESTMENTS

There are many reasons why you should watch and control your investments. One of those reasons is that if you don't measure the results, you won't be able to know if you managed to meet your goals. Another reason is that if you do not keep track of your portfolio, you will not be able to know if you are earning or losing money. Therefore, you will not know which are the investments that are leading you to success and which are those investments that are sinking your portfolio. However, one of the most important reasons why you need to keep track of your investments is that it will allow you to make essential adjustments to your portfolio. You must remember what we said in the previous chapter about the 80/20 principle, which states that 80% of your results will come from 20% of your investments. So, when you keep track of your portfolio, you will be able to identify which of the investments that are making you money and the ones that are losing money. Of course, the ones that are making you money should still be in your portfolio. However, all those investments that are losing money should be removed from your portfolio unless you identify that this loss of money is only temporary. That is, many times, there will be investments that are going through a bad time, and therefore, you must have enough emotional intelligence and patience to wait for the situation to reverse. However, on many other occasions, there will simply be investments that are destined to fail and those you must throw out of your portfolio before it is too late.

METHODS AND TOOLS FOR TRACKING INVESTMENTS

Many people believe that it is complicated to maintain constant control and monitoring over their finances, but the truth is that this is quite easy and can be done quickly with just a computer. Often when people think about how they should monitor their investments, they believe that they should be looking at financial charts all day and listening to all the news regarding the stock market when, in reality, this process should only take a few minutes. In fact, it is possible that most of the programs that you are going to see next, you already use them for many other things on a daily basis, so it is very likely that you are already used to or familiar with each of these programs.

Excel and Google Sheets

Without a doubt, Excel is one of the most used programs by people around the world since it has a wide range of uses and allows people to keep statistics, controls, data, budgets, or other similar items in an orderly way. For example, in an Excel spreadsheet, you can record your entire portfolio since you have different pages that you can use to keep your records. Ideally, you should put the name of the investment at the beginning and then put the amount of money you have invested there. Followed by the initial price of your investment, the price movements it has had from month to month and the date on which you made that investment. And finally, the amount you bought (in case they are bonds or stocks). Your objective with that investment and anything else that you think will help you correctly monitor each of your investments. You can do the same thing using Google Sheets, which have formulas and functions quite similar to those of Excel. The important thing is that you input all the data of those investments that you consider relevant. So that this data can help you adjust those investments and see which ones are earning you money and which ones you simply have to get rid of. Of course, it is not enough to do it and forget about it—you have to adjust and update it from time to time so that all that data you entered does not become obsolete. Remember, the world of investments is totally dynamic.

Automated Tracking

Of course, when you are investing through an online broker such as Robinhood, Acorns, Stash, or any of those platforms, you will not need to keep track in Excel. Since those same platforms will be in charge of providing you with all the information and updated information about each of your investments. Best of all, these applications are characterized by synthesizing information and displaying it in a way that everyone can understand, so you won't have any problems controlling your portfolio through any of these platforms. You are not restricted to online brokers for this. You can also use the services of other financial platforms such as Yahoo!, Finance, Bloomberg or Zacks, which, with a low-cost membership, will allow you to have control over your investment portfolio. Even better, they will summarize the entire process because this control will be automated. It does not matter which of these mechanisms or platforms you use. Still, you should know that it is always important to properly monitor each of your investments. Otherwise, you will never know if you are doing well or whether you have to change certain things about your investment strategy.

Segue: In the world of investing, it's not a sign of incompetence to seek out advice from professionals. In fact, this is standard practice. In the next chapter, you'll learn everything you need to get the best advice on how to pick, tract, and manage your investments.

7

SEEKING INVESTMENT ADVICE AND SERVICES

There are many people who do not have enough knowledge or experience to invest successfully on an individual basis. That is why it is often beneficial to have a financial advisor who helps with all those investment issues and the management of your money. But, of course, you must be careful when choosing the person who is going to help you with your investments; some people claim to be financial advisors but are not qualified to do so. Of course, many good financial advisors are out there, but you need to know how to find them. That is why the main objective of this chapter is for you to learn everything related to financial advisors and how you can get the best without having to incur very high fees, which is what often makes hiring a financial advisor so difficult and unattractive.

HOW TO FIND A FINANCIAL ADVISOR

Often the most complicated parts of the investment world tend to be how to get the right advisor. The most common way to find a good financial advisor is through the recommendation of a family member or friend who has done well with that advisor. However, this will not ensure that this advisor is necessarily the ideal one for you since this will depend on many things, but at least it serves as a starting point in your search. In the same way, through online databases or Google ads, you can find many options and ads about hundreds of financial advisors near your residential area. Or, if you prefer, those who work online, which will allow you to have access to them from anywhere in the world and at any time.

WHAT TO LOOK FOR IN AN ADVISOR

There are many things that are important to keep in mind when hiring a financial advisor. Many times, people hire any lawyer or any person simply because they are financial experts. Still, the truth is that this process is much more complex, and you must be much more careful. This will be the person you are going to trust with your financial future as they will be in charge of managing your investments or simply giving you the investment advice, you need. In the same way, you should know those good financial advisors are not the ones who only tell you what you want to hear.

But are also in charge of guiding you along the best path, even if it is not what you initially had in mind. One of the most important things that you must take into account when hiring a financial advisor is all those certificates or verifiable experiences they have. It is not enough to simply have a fancy office or excellent advertisements; these financial advisors must be adequately prepared to assume such responsibilities. They must also show you the results they have achieved with previous clients. This entails providing you with information about past performance and even their own experience in the field of investments. Many financial advisors have a wide lexicon and are capable of involving anyone in a game of words, but what you should really care about are the results and returns that the financial advisor can achieve. For this reason, they must show you what they can do.

It is also vital that you take into account the commission structure charged by that financial advisor. There are many who charge a percentage for each transaction made, there are others who charge a monthly fee, there are the ones who charge a flat yearly fee, and there are others who simply take a part of your earnings, but only when you have positive returns. The latter is usually the best in terms of the costs and interest involved since these financial advisors will really strive to earn you money as it is the only way for them to earn money as well. However, there are many other financial advisors who simply charge investors a commission, regardless of whether they win or lose, which is bad since then those advisors will not be motivated to make money for you because they will still have a guaranteed commission. Unfortunately, many people do not consider this factor very important, especially since financial advisors charge commissions that seem very small on the total capital invested. However, suppose you add up each of those commissions and expenses paid. In that case, you will realize that it ends up significantly reducing your profit percentage, and in some cases, it can even mean a loss of money.

For example, suppose you are going to invest $10,000 with the help of a financial advisor who charges a fixed commission of three per cent per year, plus a special fee of one per cent for transactions or changes made in the portfolio. This means that assuming that a financial advisor takes four per cent of your capital annually, he would be taking $400. As you can see, it does not matter if you earned or lost money because those fees are fixed regardless of whatever happens. This means that if you were earning a positive return on your investments of eight per cent per year, you would only be earning four per cent, which means your earnings dropped from $800 to $400. That is why you must try to find financial advisors who have a better fee structure. Otherwise, your profits could decrease a lot. Likewise, many people think that using financial advisors will ensure their success, but the truth is that this is not always the case. In fact, it is proven that most financial advisors do not exceed the average return of the market, which is eight per cent, meaning that you would earn more and spend less investing in an index fund on your own. However, financial advisors can benefit all those who do not feel confident enough to start investing without the help of professionals.

Segue: You're all set! In the next few chapters, you will learn the best approaches to investing in specific low-risk (and a couple of medium-risk) investment options.

8

MONEY MARKET ACCOUNTS

In this third part of the book, you will learn in-depth about all those financial assets and low- and medium-risk investment mechanisms in which you can start investing immediately. Best of all, each of these investment methods that we will evaluate is very easy to start investing in. For most of them, you will simply need the help of your computer, your knowledge, and of course, the money you are willing to invest. In this chapter, you will learn about money market accounts. These are very different from the savings accounts that people usually have and do not generate as many returns. However, this is one of the investment mechanisms that have the lowest risks of all that we are going to see, so it can be very beneficial for you to learn the characteristics of these accounts and see if they can be suitable for achieving your long-term financial goals.

WHAT IS IT, AND HOW DOES IT WORK?

A money market account works in a similar way as a savings account, but with the difference that it pays a much higher interest rate on your savings since those savings rates are the same as those established in the money markets, which usually can be much higher than those traditionally offered by banks. Therefore, many people are attracted to this investment instrument; as you can see, it is totally easy to do and has very low costs since opening these accounts is usually free. However, it has a small barrier to entry. Money market accounts often require a minimum amount of money to be invested, which will vary depending on the financial platform. In the same way, the conditions to withdraw your money can often be a little different from what a traditional savings account would have. That is, when your money is in a traditional bank account, you can withdraw it whenever you want since there is no minimum amount that you have to withdraw. On the other hand, when it comes to a money market account, many of these platforms require that a minimum amount be withdrawn only after a minimum period of time has passed since you deposited your money.

WHAT MAKES IT LOW-RISK?

Money markets are among the safest investments that you will be able to find in the market for many reasons. In the first place, there is no volatility involved. That is, they will pay you a fixed percentage of money for your interest, regardless of what is happening economically or financially in the world of investments. On the other hand, other types of investments may depend on the volatility in the market at a given time, making that type of investment riskier than money markets. In addition, you should know that when you invest in this type of account, your money is fully insured. So, it is almost impossible for fraud or anything else to occur that puts your money at risk. That is why if you are looking for an investment that is entirely risk-free (or at least the risks they have are very few) and that also provides passive income on a constant basis, money market accounts can be an excellent option.

ADVANTAGES OF THIS INVESTMENT

One of the most significant advantages of money markets is that you will have excellent compound interest on your capital, which will make your money multiply exponentially. This is not achieved by all investments since not all of them provide passive income to investors. Another great advantage is that everyone can access a money market account, unlike other investments where there can be many barriers to entry, or you have to have a lot of money to invest. Best of all, what most attracts the attention of many investors worldwide, is that your money will be safe since it will not depend on the momentary volatility of the market. That is why if you are not very risk-tolerant, but you still want your savings to start multiplying, this is an excellent option for you.

Disadvantages

Although money markets are a fairly safe type of investment and have many advantages to offer you, it is also essential that you understand the disadvantages of this type of investment. One of those disadvantages, and probably the one that makes many investors avoid investing here, is that you will not be protected against inflation. This is because it is a fixed-income financial asset, which will always grant the same percentage of interest on your money. This is totally positive if we live in a world where inflation does not exist. Still, since that does not happen, often, those interest rates end up being lower than the annual inflation percentage. For example, if your money market account offers returns of 12% per year, but the inflation percentage is 13%. You will be losing money, apart from the fact that that money will be parked there for the term of the investment.

On the other hand, with other financial assets that appreciate over time, such as stocks, you will be protected against inflation because they are not fixed-income financial assets. Of course, that is why money markets should not be your only investment; as you have learned throughout this book, you should always have a diversified portfolio. Nevertheless, they are a good option to consider and include in your portfolio if you want to give it a little more stability.

WHERE YOU CAN START INVESTING

You are probably wondering where you can start investing in money market accounts at this time. The answer is that there are many providers of this type of investment on the Internet. The best known are Zynlo and Quontic, which are two financial platforms that offer this type of account to investors of all kinds. Best of all, you can access these accounts easily and for free in a matter of seconds. The important thing is that you compare the costs involved in each of them, as well as which platform offers the best interest rate for your money.

Segue: Next, you'll learn everything you need to know about investing in high-yield, low-risk savings accounts.

9

HIGH-YIELD SAVINGS ACCOUNT

Many so-called experts in the investment world will tell you that a high-yield savings account is not a proper investment mechanism since they see it as a waste of time and totally unnecessary. However, if you are one of those people who do not like to take many risks and do not prioritize getting exponential profits, you can settle for small profits as long as your money is safe. In that case, then this is an excellent option for you. This type of investment consists of putting your money in an account that generates a high level of interest on that money. But the difference is that you will be able to manage it like a traditional bank account since you will be able to withdraw and use your money whenever you want. That is why it would be a mistake to confuse the high-yield savings account with the money market account

—they are two different things. Money market accounts are designed in a way that you can't immediately withdraw or use your money, unlike high-yield savings accounts that have much more liquidity.

The big difference between this type of investment and traditional bank accounts is that high-yield savings account pays a much higher interest rate, as well as offer other benefits such as quick and easy online transactions. Fortunately, many times the platforms that provide this type of service are usually as safe as traditional banks, where it is almost impossible for there to be any fraud or circumstance that causes you to lose your money. The point is that these types of accounts allow people to obtain a high interest in their savings. In addition, it is a low-risk investment mechanism since it does not affect market volatility.

ADVANTAGES

One of the best advantages offered by high-yield savings accounts is that your money will not be put at risk since your investment will not depend on market volatility but will be well-protected. In addition, there is the advantage that you have a fixed income assured since you will receive passive income as interest from time to time. Another benefit is that you will be able to enjoy your savings at the same time that you invest since you will be able to use them to do whatever you want with that money, something that cannot be done through many other mechanisms. However, it has the enormous disadvantage that it will not protect you against inflation since, although it is a safe investment and you can withdraw your money whenever you want, the interest rates are fixed and do not change frequently, and they do not usually beat inflation. Therefore, if you live in a high-inflation country, it is good to first look at other alternatives before deciding on a high-yield savings account.

HOW TO GET STARTED

Next, we will look at some of the factors you should look for in a high-yield account if you truly want to make a good profit and make your money work for you. One of the things you should look for is that the account you are going to open offers an interest rate that is much higher than the national reference rates (the rates established by banks). In fact, and as it may seem incredible, some high-yield accounts offer rates up to 20 times higher than the national reference rates. They do this in order to compete with other types of traditional investment mechanisms such as bonds. In the same way, it is important that you pay attention to each of the specific conditions and terms of those companies that offer this type of account since they will be necessary when withdrawing your money, making deposits, and receiving payments. Therefore, you must not open a high-yield savings account without carefully reading all its terms and conditions; otherwise, you could get some unpleasant surprises. In the same way, you should know that many of these platforms are online-only banks, so it is very likely that you will not have any institution or branch to go to in the event that an issue arises, or you have doubts about something. In general, that is not usually a problem, but it is still important that you know it.

WHERE TO INVEST

Axos, CIBC Agility, and Marcus by Goldman Sachs are some of the many options where you can start investing in high-yield savings account quickly, safely, and easily. Each of these platforms works only online, and they have the advantage that there are very few requirements for you to start investing with them. What you should keep in mind is that it is helpful that you read the terms and conditions of each of these platforms beforehand so that you know what investment mechanisms those platforms use. Of course, there are many other high-yield saving accounts that can be used apart from the ones mentioned above. But these are the best-known and therefore preferred by investors worldwide. Many people do not have security and confidence in these types of platforms since they consider them to be very risky as they only work online. However, often these platforms can be even more secure than traditional banks since they are usually decentralized or have much less bureaucracy.

That is why you should not worry about the fact that these platforms are decentralized because your money will be well protected and will multiply little by little over time.

Segue: Next, you'll learn everything you need to know about investing in low-risk cash management accounts.

10

CASH MANAGEMENT ACCOUNTS

Although very few people know about this innovative and safe investment method, there is something called cash management accounts that are good for those investors who want to take a little risk and at the same time obtain some profits and passive income. These types of investments are offered by brokerage firms as well as Robo-advisers. This represents a great alternative to the traditional banking system where we keep our money since, with a cash management account, the broker will automatically manage and divide your money so that it yields much more, something that is not possible through a traditional bank. Basically, this type of investment keeps the money of investors who want to invest large sums of money safe since it will not only have good returns and receive interest, but it is also eligible for coverage under the Federal Deposit Insurance Corp. (FDIC). However, this type of investment may not be as attractive for those investors who seek to invest only a small amount of money since this is an investment mechanism that does not pay as much interest but instead focuses on diversifying your money and keeping it safe while generating some returns.

HOW DO THEY WORK?

When you put your money in a traditional bank, the bank will store your money. You can then have it available whenever you want through debit cards or cash withdrawals. In other words, traditional banks do not only pay very little interest on your money; they don't do anything with that money so that it grows for you. This is the main difference between cash management accounts and traditional banks. Through a cash management account, your money is divided among different banks and investment portfolios. Each of these amounts will be insured and generate a higher percentage of interest. This all happens automatically, so you don't have to worry about any of those factors.

In the same way, all that money will be available quickly in your account, so even though your money will be divided into many parts, you will be able to access that money in one place. This is one of the many advantages that cash management accounts offer you. For example, if you deposit

$300,000 into your account, it might automatically divide it into five amounts of $60,000 that will be sent to different banking or financial institutions. That money will then start earning interest, apart from the fact that, as we said before, it will be insured.

This means that you will only need a computer or smartphone, as well as a payment method accepted by each of these platforms, to start investing. Furthermore, as you can see, since these investment methods are safe and straightforward, they can be ideal for all types of investors. Finally, it is also important to know that, despite the fact that your money will be divided into multiple sectors, you will be able to access that money quickly and automatically whenever you want.

ADVANTAGES

Among the different advantages offered by cash management accounts is that you will have a fast and simple way to invest. Which does not require any type of analysis or anything complex since it is simply depositing your money and waiting for it to generate income. Similarly, this type of account offers a much more attractive interest rate than that provided by traditional banks or some alternative investment platforms, so it can be a perfect option when it comes to diversifying your portfolio.

Disadvantages

One of the disadvantages of this type of investment is that it does not offer as many returns as other investment mechanisms do. This is because your money will be parked in the cash management account, and you have to invest a lot of money to see an actual return that will be worth the time. So, this may not be the best option if you are looking to get high returns for little capital. Another disadvantage is that it only works online and, although many people do not have problems with this, there are others who like to have a branch to go to in case of any problem. In addition, this type of investment has few alternatives to offer within its platforms. That is, with many online brokers, you can buy stocks, bonds, or invest in cryptocurrencies or any other financial asset. With a cash management account, you are not able to do any of that since you will only be able to deposit your money, use it, and see how that money earns interest and generates passive income over time.

WHERE TO INVEST IN CASH MANAGEMENT ACCOUNTS

Currently, there are many financial platforms such as Fidelity, Robinhood, and Betterment that offer this type of service, as well as many others that help make these platforms much more complete. In this way, people cannot only have cash management accounts, but they also have access to funds to invest in many other financial assets; accordingly, you will be able to diversify your portfolio much more, which is always essential.

Segue: Next, you'll learn everything you need to know about in low-risk and high-yield certificates of deposits.

11

CERTIFICATES OF DEPOSIT

Certificates of Deposit are among the best-known and most used since investing in certificates of deposit is very easy and can be done quickly. In general, this type of investment is offered by banking institutions to their clients. It consists of a loan that the client makes to the bank, and that money will generate a fixed interest. However, most certificates of deposit only pay interest annually or at the end of the investment term. That is, if you invest your money in a certificate of deposit for a period of six months, you will receive that money you lent after six months, plus the interest that has accumulated during that time. Of course, it should be noted that each institution may have different conditions and terms. So, certificates of deposit may have different ways of being invested. However, the important thing you should know is that this is one of the most basic and safest investments that exist since there is no way for the bank not to return your money or not pay you that interest.

ADVANTAGES

The most significant advantages of this type of investment are that your money will be safe and that it is also a very low-risk investment. That is why it is considered one of the favourite investments for all those conservative investors who want to get a little more profit for their money. In addition, certificates of deposit are used so that you can obtain a fixed income from time to time. If the term of that investment is more than one year, you can then receive passive income from time to time. The important thing is that this type of investment is very safe. You also know in advance how much money you are going to earn since the bank or institution where you are making that investment will tell you exactly how much interest it will pay you. This is something that is not available in other investments since, most of the time, investors cannot know the exact amount they are going to receive from an investment due to market volatility.

CONS OF THIS INVESTMENT

You must be very careful since your money is not protected against inflation with certificates of deposit. This is because your interest rate remains fixed once you make that investment. So, if in one-year inflation is 8%, and the certificate of deposit pays 6% annually, you will be losing money. Likewise, one disadvantage that worries investors is that, generally, the interest rates offered in this type of investment do not exceed the usual market rate of return. It is currently 8%; therefore, when an investment offers returns of less than eight per cent, then it is best to look for another alternative. That is why the best option is not a certificate of deposit if you want to multiply your money exponentially or obtain large profits.

On the other hand, if you want to have your money safe and get some returns on that money, then you could make this investment. However, it should be noted that these investments should only be made for diversification. That is, you should not put all your money in this type of conservative investment since you would basically have no profit at all.

WHERE YOU CAN INVEST IN A CERTIFICATE OF DEPOSIT

Most traditional banks offer certificates of deposit (CD) to their customers. Still, you must bear in mind that it is likely that the vast majority of these banks charge some commission. So, you must check if you will continue to have profits after having paid those commissions. Many times, these commissions can be fixed or based on a percentage, depending on the amount that you are going to invest. Fixed fees are great for people who invest large amounts of money, but they are very detrimental for investors who only want to invest a small amount. The important thing is that you are aware of those commissions (if they are charged) since they can take a large part of your earnings. Unlike what used to happen before, today, you can invest in a CD from your own cell phone. This means that you don't even have to go to the bank in person because you can invest in a certificate of deposit through your bank's home banking or mobile application. Where it will tell you how much the interest rate of that CD is, the terms available, and the conditions in case you want to withdraw your investment. You must bear in mind that most banks do not allow you to withdraw your money beforehand as you will have to comply with the previously established deadline.

Many banks that work only online, like some of the platforms that we have been mentioning throughout the book, offer this type of option, with the difference that they generally offer better interest rates. Most experts recommend that while all these innovative platforms are excellent for investing in other types of financial assets, if you are going to invest in a certificate of deposit, it is best to do it through a traditional bank since these offer better options in terms of investment. However, the important thing is that you look for the platform or the investment mechanism that best suits your needs since you must remember that what is suitable for another person may not be totally appropriate for you.

WHAT THE EXPERTS SAY ABOUT THIS

Over the years, there has been a lot of controversy surrounding investment mechanisms such as certificates of deposit. This is because there are different opinions on the part of many investors and experts in the world of finance, which is why many people do not know if CDs really are a good investment option or simply a waste of time that you should avoid. For example, Robert Kiyosaki, author of many personal finance books and one of the world's most well-known investors, has repeatedly said that people should try to avoid investing in certificates of deposit because they are simply a waste of time. This is because many experts criticize the fact that no CD is able to beat the average market yield of eight per cent. This means that if you invest in an index fund or any other simple investment mechanism that is related to the stock market, you will earn much more money than you could earn with a certificate of deposit.

However, many other experts consider certificates of deposit to be almost perfect because they leave aside the aggressive volatility of the market. And focus only on fixed returns that give investors passive income without having to do anything. While this is a huge advantage, you also have to consider that everyone wants to multiply their money and that no one is going to settle for a rate of return that is lower than the average rate of return in the market.

The conclusion of all this is that these types of investments are useful if you really put together a diversified portfolio. Suppose, instead, you focus on putting all your money into this financial asset. In that case, you simply will not have the expected returns. Basically, you will be wasting a lot of time since that money could be generating a lot of returns in other types of investments.

Segue: Next, you'll learn everything you need to know about investing in low-risk treasury bonds, bills, and notes.

12

TREASURY NOTES, BILLS, AND BONDS

One of the many ways that governments around the world have of being able to finance public spending and all other state activities is through the issuance of certain financial instruments, such as treasury notes, bills, and bonds. That not only allow governments to raise a lot of money but also allow many investors to invest their money safely and quickly. Most of these investments offer an average return but with a much lower risk than other types of investments. This is because when someone invests in treasury notes, bills, or government bonds, they are investing directly through investment mechanisms that are promoted by the state. As we all know, it is impossible for the government to default and not pay its debts to investors (at least in the United States, United Kingdom and many other countries). Unlike many companies that sometimes offer corporate bonds that they cannot pay later, leaving many investors totally devastated and with great losses. These are among the most used investments by people around the world, especially by those who do not have a lot of knowledge in the area of finance and investment. Since to invest in treasury notes, bills, and bonds, you do not have to do such in-depth research, and the process is much quicker and easier.

TREASURY BILLS

Treasury bills are one of the many financial instruments issued by the government in order to raise additional funds for the construction of public schools, highways, and all the other things that are the responsibility of the federal government. These are basically loans that an investor make to the government for a short term since these bills have a period of one year or less. In fact, a treasury bill can last from a single week to 52 weeks in a year, but you must bear in mind that the longer that term, the greater the interest that you will receive for that bill. In other words, if you invest in a treasury bill with a duration of four weeks, you will receive very little interest, unlike what you would receive if you invested with a term of, for example, 40 weeks. However, there is something that needs to be clarified regarding the interest that they are going to pay you, and it is this part where many investors tend to get confused. Unlike other financial assets such as bonds, treasury bills do not pay interest from time to time; interest is paid when the final term of the investment is met. Therefore, you will be able to know in advance what the interest is or the final amount of money you will receive. This is because the face value of the treasury bill is different from the amount that the investor pays. For example, if you buy a treasury bill with a face value of $2,000, you will probably only have to pay $1,800. At the end of the term, you will receive the $2,000 face value (which includes your $200 profit).

Similarly, you must remember that, unlike many other financial assets where the amounts to invest vary drastically, treasury bills are issued in amounts of $1,000 and up. That is, they can be from $1,000 to $5,000,000, but always keep that figure as a reference. One of the most significant advantages of these investment mechanisms is that people will be investing in something extremely safe since it will be backed by the Treasury Department. In addition, you will be able to know in advance how much your profit will be, so you will have a more exact parameter to evaluate that investment and make your final decision. However, one of the most attractive aspects of these investments is that the amount of interest you receive will be tax-exempt (at least in most states). So, unlike many other investments, that profit will be net. Of course, it is always crucial that you consult the local laws on the taxes to be paid to avoid any problems in the future. Treasury bills can be purchased through an online broker or directly through the TreasuryDirect website. In general, buying them from the TreasuryDirect page is recommended because it implies fewer expenses unless you have an account with an online broker that does not charge commissions for transactions.

TREASURY NOTES

Treasury notes, unlike treasury bills, are long-term investment instruments, with a minimum term of 2 years and a maximum term of 10 years. These are also payable debts generated by the government so that many investors can invest quickly and safely. They are characterized by having a fixed interest rate that will be paid from time to time, depending on the term that the investment lasts. In general, interest is paid every six months until the completion period is met. In other words, you will receive at least four installments with your earnings as interest, and the maximum interest you can receive is 20 fixed installments. The vast majority of treasury notes have adjustable interest rates, which means that in the event of a period of inflation or economic crisis, the interest rate that you are going to receive could increase. So, these treasury notes are much more competitive, and thus investors feel genuinely attracted. However, it will also depend on the duration of that investment. Treasury notes are

also known as one of the safest long-term investments on the market since, as we have said before, everything that is directly backed by any government is very safe. If you want to add a financial asset to your portfolio that generates a fixed income from time to time and that also has a fairly low-risk rate. In that case, treasury notes are an excellent option.

TREASURY BONDS

On the other hand, Treasury bonds are long-term investments that investors can make by making a loan to the government. However, you should keep in mind that the vast majority of these bonds have a tenure of up to 30 years, so basically, they are suitable investments to make when you are young but not a good option as you age. As expected, thanks to the long-term of these bonds, they usually offer interest rates that are quite attractive. In theory, it is a very safe investment mechanism since it is impossible for the Federal Reserve to go bankrupt. That is why it is usually said that there is no risk involved in this type of investment, something that is very rare to achieve in today's world of finance, where there are so many investment mechanisms that are very volatile. The vast majority of these bonds pay interest every six months, so you will receive passive income from time to time along with those bonds. Of course, you do not have to keep your investment for ten years, since after 45 days, they can be sold on the secondary market. However, if you do this, then automatically, you won't earn any money, but rather, you will have wasted all that time you put your money into the bonds. That is why for this type of investment, which is so safe, a lot of patience is required, since otherwise, you will not have good returns.

The profitability of government bonds is related to the credit rating, which is the ability of the issuer to pay the debt. The worse the credit rating, the higher the risk and the higher the return must be offered for the investment to be interesting. The good thing is that the vast majority of governments have excellent credit ratings, so it is almost impossible for them not to pay the money to investors. However, we must always be aware of the probability that governments can fall into financial default, although this should not be a problem in powerful countries. The evolution of interest rates is the factor that most affects the yield of government bonds. If interest rates rise, new bond issues will increase their issue rates, offering higher returns. If, on the other hand, interest rates fall, the new bonds will have lower yields. To reduce the risk related to the evolution of interest rates, securities with repayment terms compatible with the financial objectives of the investment can be contracted. As you can see, investing in government bonds allows the investor to opt for a safe investment with a predictable income stream. Finally, to have an opportunity to invest in society, since this type of investment is considered low risk.

ARE THESE INVESTMENTS REALLY SAFE?

Yes. In fact, we could say that there are no safer investments in the market than all those mentioned above. However, this does not mean that you should not seek out all the information necessary to ensure that these investment mechanisms are aligned with your objectives. Otherwise, you could end up with some unpleasant surprises. For example, when you are going to invest in treasury bills, notes, or bonds, you must make sure that you fully understand how they work. Many people invest in these just for the fact that they are safe and there are no risks involved. And then they do not understand that these financial assets do not have as much liquidity. Therefore, they may not end up being as easy to sell or regain their initial investment.

ADVANTAGES OF THESE INVESTMENTS

These types of investments (treasury notes, bills, and bonds) offer many advantages, such as the fact that each of them is risk-free and will give you passive income from time to time or simply some safe percentage of profit. This does not happen with many other financial instruments, so in this way, you will be ensuring that you will get your money back quickly and safely. In addition, they have the advantage of being very easy to obtain since they can be purchased through the secondary market (that is, through online brokers) or directly through the websites authorized by the Treasury Department.

WHAT ABOUT INFLATION?

The negative side of this type of investment is that almost none of these financial assets is capable of outperforming annual inflation. Of course, when inflation is low or stable, generally, each of these financial assets offers quite attractive interest rates for investors, but when inflation is relatively high worldwide, they do not usually generate the expected returns. You must remember that the benchmark rate of return is usually eight per cent, as that is what the market has shown it can deliver in a typical year. Of course, it can be more or less, but that is the percentage that the market return usually approaches. Therefore, if any of these investment mechanisms that we talk about in this chapter does not come close to that eight per cent return. Then it is better that you look at any other of the options available in the market that can generate you really good returns, apart from protecting yourself from inflation. However, you should keep in mind that, in these cases, the level of risk is going to increase.

BONDS OR STOCKS?

For a long time, people have wondered which investment is better: bonds or stocks. But, alas, this is a complex question that does not have a single answer since it will depend on what your long-term goals are when it comes to investing. For example, suppose you want to obtain a fixed income and put your savings to work little by little. In that case, the ideal is that you invest your money in bonds because, apart from being low risk, they will provide you with passive income. In fact, bonds are generally more frequently recommended for older people as these people tend to have a better risk tolerance.

On the other hand, if what you are looking for is to multiply your money exponentially and start building generational wealth, then stocks are a better option. Of course, it does not mean that if you invest in one, you cannot invest in the other since the ideal is that you put together a genuinely diversified portfolio to protect yourself against market volatility. But unfortunately, what happens with many people is that they want to put all their money in stocks, bonds, or any other financial asset, which makes them leave everything in the hands of just one industry or just one investment—a sure formula for failure. That is why great investors know how to combine both types of investments.

Segue: Next, you'll learn all you need to know about low-risk corporate bonds.

13

CORPORATE BONDS

In the preceding chapter, you saw some ways that governments around the world obtain income in order to finance public spending and be able to build schools, improve highways, improve security and many other things that are in charge of the government. However, companies often also need to raise money from investors around the world in order to continue expanding, improving, reaching new customers, and so on. One of the ways that enable companies to do this is through the issuance of stocks. However, many times this is not enough since companies need much capital to carry out all these projects. That is why some companies (especially large ones with a long history) issue corporate bonds. These work in a similar way to government bonds; the difference is that, instead of being backed by the government, they are backed by the company that issues them. But the operation is the same. The investor pays an amount of money that goes to the company, receives interest from time to time, and at the end of the term of that bond, the total amount of money invested will be returned to them. They will have earned interest during all that time.

Corporate bonds generally offer better rates of return than government bonds, but that doesn't mean they will have incredible rates of return. In other words, this type of bond will continue to be part of the conservative investment group. And is ideal for those investors who do not want to take as many risks or simply do not want to invest in more volatile investment mechanisms. The problem is that many people think that by investing in corporate bonds issued by large companies, they will be able to enjoy the same benefits that the shareholders of those same companies enjoy; the fact is that it is something totally different. That is, suppose you buy a corporate bond in Apple. That bond will not generate the same returns as Apple stocks, even if it is the same company. This is because although with the bond, you will have passive income in a stable and continuous way, with the stocks, you would have the advantage that they can rise in price and generate exponential profits. Of course, it does not mean that one investment is better than the other since that will depend on the individual interests of each investor, but you must bear in mind that these are totally different things even though they belong to the same company.

THE RISKS OF THESE INVESTMENTS

One of the biggest concerns that exist when investing in corporate bonds is that there are many companies that are not in a good economic position and therefore cannot meet their debts. That is, many people are attracted to some corporate bonds that offer very high yields, but the truth is that this implies that the risks involved are quite high as well. That is why there are many financial agencies that are responsible for granting a rating to each of these bonds, such as Moody's and S&P. Each bond is given a rating that can range from AAA (which is the best rating that a bond can obtain), followed by AA, A, BBB, BB, B, CCC, CC and C. For example, a bond that has a BBB rating tends to offer good returns but has a moderate level of risk. In contrast, an AAA-rated bond means it is very safe, as the company is unlikely to default or go bankrupt. However, the reward level will also be low; CCC-rated bonds are very risky as they often belong to companies that are in a terrible financial position or going out of business, so they offer incredible returns to try to attract many investors and thus be able to save themselves. So, of course, these types of bonds should be avoided, even if they promise incredible returns.

BE CAREFUL WITH JUNK BONDS

In the same way, around corporate bonds, there are usually many junk bonds that companies offer to investors where they promise very high returns and low risk, but the truth is that most of the time, these bonds are not backed by anything, which is why they really have no value. Of course, large companies with a long history would never do that. Still, many times there are start-ups that grow very quickly and urgently need to raise capital to continue expanding and avoid collapsing. Often, these companies issue a series of junk bonds with the intent to attract the attention of many investors, which you should avoid. Junk bonds usually end up being very risky, despite being told otherwise at first, since although they are totally legal, they do not explain their operation and conditions well. Hence, they usually end up being harmful to the portfolio of the junk bond investors. That is why, if you really want to optimize your portfolio, you should stay away from junk bonds.

In fact, one of the causes of the tremendous economic crisis that occurred worldwide in 2008 was the high issuance of junk bonds. This happened because often, people have a hard time recognizing a junk bond since these have the aspects of normal bonds but can have poisonous portions. However, that year, the main financial institutions knew that people were willing to invest their money since everyone saw that the stock market was going through an excellent period and that nothing was going to stop it. So those financial institutions took advantage and started issuing a series of derivative financial mechanisms and instruments, so at that time, you could buy bonds that were derivatives of other bonds, which is complete madness. That is why when that bubble burst, the great crisis that we all know as the subprime crisis was generated, which left millions of people around the world unemployed, and in enormous despair. So, therefore, if you are going to invest in corporate bonds, you must make sure that they are not derivatives of other bonds. And that they have the structure that we have been explaining throughout the book since otherwise, your money could be in great danger.

How to Recognize a Junk Bond

There are three fundamental factors that will help you recognize those junk bonds that are being offered in the market. One of those factors is the risk rate. You can determine the risk rate by taking into account the ratings that the bond has. If a bond has a CCC rating, it is very likely to have too high a risk ratio, which is one of the first indications that it could be a junk bond. The second factor is the high fees. When a bond charges too many commissions or has very high fees, it is because the company or institution that issues it knows that it needs to raise as much money as possible before it is too late. The second red flag is when a bond charges you too much commission. Finally, you must take into account the rate of return of that bond. Many times, in the world of finance, the phrase is repeated that something is too good to be true; in most cases, what seems to be too good ends up being some kind of scam. In the world of investments, the risks are at the same level as the rewards, so if you invest in something that promises to give you exponential returns that seem implausible, it is likely that the risk is so high that it is better that you invest in another financial instrument.

WHAT ARE THE BEST CORPORATE BONDS TO BUY?

Corporate bonds are not the investments that will make you a millionaire, but they can help you build a well-diversified investment portfolio. In this chapter, we will show you some of the companies that currently issue the best corporate bonds. One such company is the world-famous Boeing. This company is recognized worldwide for being a leading manufacturer of aircraft as well as of aircraft parts used by other companies. Undoubtedly, this is one of the companies that leads the stock market and has enormous purchasing power, making it one of the most valuable companies in the world. Boeing is not only recognized for its great capacity when it comes to assembling airplanes, but it also offers one of the best corporate bonds on the market, currently with an interest rate of over four per cent and interest payments every six months. S&P gives it a BBB rating because although it is a very safe company with a high economic level, bonds that offer high rates of return like this tend to have higher risks. Another of these companies is CVS Health Corporation, which is known to be one of the leaders in the pharmaceutical sector in the United States.

We all know how excellent its products are and how much we can get at each of its branches. However, few people know how attractive the corporate bonds of this company are, so it may be very good for you to take a look. CVS offers a corporate bond that has an interest rate greater than four per cent, and what is truly incredible is that this interest rate exceeds the dividend rate that the same company offers to shareholders, which is two per cent. Without a doubt, CVS is not only an excellent solution when you need some medication, but it is also an excellent option for all those who seek to balance their portfolio through corporate bonds. McDonald's also offers one of the best corporate bonds out there. As we all know, McDonald's is a company that generates a lot of money annually but still needs to issue bonds that allow it to have a much higher cash flow. McDonald's stocks have always been characterized by being stable and offering good dividends. Its corporate bonds are no exception, as they are one of the favorites of diversified investors worldwide.

The interest rate offered by this company to investors with its corporate bonds is more than four per cent, higher than the percentage of dividends it pays to shareholders, which is currently 2.48%. However, keep in mind that McDonald's recently had to close more than 850 franchises that were in Russian territory due to the war with Ukraine, so many investors are concerned that this could create a cash flow problem for the company. However, experts say not to worry, as McDonald's has the purchasing power and sales level to meet each of its long-term obligations. Finally, one of the best options when it comes to choosing a corporate bond is the FedEx Corporation. This is a company that moves a lot of money; it needs a lot of working capital and is currently offering an interest rate of 4.28%. Which is one of the best rates of return that you will be able to find in the market. That's why FedEx not only takes care of bringing shipments directly to your door, but it can also take care of making you passive income easily from time to time.

ARE CORPORATE BONDS REALLY A GOOD INVESTMENT?

This answer will depend on the long-term financial goals that each person has. What is safe to say is that the returns generated by corporate bonds are going to be much lower than those that can be generated by instruments such as stocks, mutual funds, or other investments that are a little riskier but offer better returns. That is why before investing in a corporate bond, you must evaluate if it is really worth it. The companies named earlier have some of the best rates of return in the corporate bond market, but they still don't get above four per cent return. This is very little compared to the average market return of eight per cent. There are many experts who consider that it is much better for you to invest in other financial assets that also generate passive income, such as dividend stocks, which we will review in chapter 15. However, if you are looking for a secure option where to put your money and, at the same time, that generates some returns (even if they are low), then do not doubt that corporate bonds can be a good option. The good thing about the stock market and the world of investments is that there will always be options for everyone; depending on the different objectives that each person has, anyone can invest effectively as long as they know how to do it.

Segue: In the next chapter, you'll learn what you need to know about investing in low-risk preferred stocks.

14

PREFERRED STOCKS

Preferred stocks are issued by companies or institutions, which, unlike common stocks, have specific priorities over other shareholders. However, you should know that holding a preferred stock of a company does not mean that you will obtain higher profits or that you will have a vote in the shareholders' meeting, but rather that you will have priority in dividend payments, as long as the company issues them. Similarly, a preferred stock assures you that you will be a priority if a company is in financial trouble and cannot meet its dividend payments. Since people with common stocks will have much less opportunity to receive those payments.

Preferred stocks have a fixed or variable dividend agreed with their purchasers, which should not be confused with a fixed income coupon. It is a dividend, and, as such, if the company does not obtain benefits, it does not have an obligation to pay it on the previously stipulated dates. Like ordinary stocks, preferred stocks do not have a stipulated maturity date as they are issued in perpetuity. Although the issuer may decide to repurchase them based on the characteristics of the issue and on the dates established in advance.

IS IT REALLY WORTH IT?

Many people often wonder if it is worth investing in preferred stocks, and the truth is that you are not going to get a lot of profit through these financial assets. In other words, the volatility that you are going to face is going to be the same. The market value of the stock is going to be the same as that of a common stock, with the difference being that, in order to receive that priority, we were talking about earlier, you will have to pay a little more. Of course, you will also have the enormous advantage that these stocks will be long-term because they don't have a due date but offer constant interest rates. Therefore, you will be able to receive passive income throughout your life. However, it should be noted that the return percentage offered by these preferred stocks is usually very low, so considering the cost and likely rewards, it is probably not worth it. Similarly, investing in a preferred stock carries a high financial risk since these companies probably have financial problems and therefore have to issue this type of stock in order to raise much more money quickly and easily. In other words, there is no doubt that between a common stock and a preferred stock, the ideal is for all novice investors to choose common stocks.

Segue: Next you'll learn everything you should know about investing in low-risk dividend stocks.

15

DIVIDEND STOCKS

In the first chapters, you learned how the stock market works. Specifically, what stocks are and why they bring many benefits to investors. There are many types of stocks, such as income stocks, growth stocks, defensive stocks, and many others. But one of the most important (and at the same time, one of the most underrated in the market) is dividend stocks. These are all those stocks issued by companies that pay dividends from time to time, and usually, that dividend payment term is made quarterly, every four months, semi-annually or annually. These dividends not only allow you to continuously reinvest your money but also allow you to generate passive income and take advantage of the good results that the company is achieving. However, you should keep in mind that not all companies issue dividends, which does not mean that it is a bad thing.

Similarly, it is not unusual for a company to issue dividends: these are two positions that companies take depending on the current situation they have and their future projects. For example, Tesla is a company that has grown rapidly over the last decade, and it is a company that has shown incredible returns on the stock market. In 2017, Tesla stock had a market value of $70, and today it is worth more than $800. In addition, this is one of the companies that generate the most money annually in the world, making the great Elon Musk the wealthiest person on the planet.

However, despite all the economic success that the company has had, it has never started a dividend policy. Since it argues that it is better to use all that capital to continue expanding its operations and its customer base while focusing on increasing annual production. The same has happened with other fast-growing companies such as Amazon. However, other companies such as McDonald's or Coca-Cola, which have a long history in the market and generate a lot of money annually, decided to have a dividend policy a long time ago. They do this as a way to reward their shareholders, who, apart from seeing how the value of those stocks increases over time, also receive passive income. Likewise, this is beneficial for these companies from an accounting point of view since those dividends they pay are accounted for as expenses and, therefore, can be a tax aid for these companies. What this means is that companies that issue dividends are not better than those that do not pay dividends, nor vice versa. These are decisions that companies make based on different factors since what each of these companies wants is to continue growing and expanding their production and their level of sales. However, for you, dividend stocks can be an excellent option where you can generate passive income and then capital gains through those stocks, so you can earn additional profit.

DIVIDEND ARISTOCRATS

Within dividend stocks, there are two groups of classifications: dividend aristocrats and dividend kings. These are classified in one way or another depending on the number of years in which the company has continuously issued dividends and uninterruptedly. In the case of the aristocrats, those companies have issued dividends for at least 25 consecutive years. This is undoubtedly a considerable amount of time, and they are usually companies with an excellent track record in the market. They generate a lot of confidence in investors because they know that these companies with such a long track record will continue to stand firm and lead each of their sectors and industries. Some of the dividend aristocrats that we can name are: Unilever, Pepsi, Caterpillar, Fresenius, Chevron, and AT&T. As you can see, each of these companies is widely recognized worldwide, and they have the advantage that if you invest in them, you will receive passive income steadily for a long time. You will be able to reinvest that money, and you will also be able to earn capital gains when you decide to sell those stocks.

DIVIDEND KINGS

On the other hand, when we talk about dividend kings, we refer to all those stocks of companies that have issued dividends for at least 50 years. These are usually already historic companies and can even be among the most valuable companies in the world. Within the dividend kings, you will find some important companies such as Colgate, 3M, Target, Lowe's, P&G, and Coca-Cola. And many other companies that have maintained an incredible trajectory in the stock market since it is obviously not easy to continue delivering dividends to shareholders for at least 50 years. The important thing about all this is that these are usually very reliable companies that generate outstanding returns for investors. Since the percentage of dividends is also usually quite high. Of course, a stock of a company that does not offer dividends can have much higher yields than a company that does issue dividends. Still, it is important to know that dividends will serve as a source of passive income. Ensuring that you will be able to reinvest all that money later so that your money can multiply exponentially more easily.

DEFENSIVE STOCKS

Defensive stocks are divided into those that grant dividends as well as other classifications that are commonly given to stocks according to the type of company. Defensive stocks are those that belong to stable companies and have little market volatility. In general, these stocks belong to very well-known companies with an impeccable track record in the market. However, it should be noted that since they are not volatile companies, there will also be little chance that the price of these stocks will increase. Therefore, enabling you to obtain large profits. Some defensive stocks that you can get in the market are Coca-Cola, P&G, Ford, CVS, and many others.

GROWTH STOCKS

Growth stocks are those belonging to companies that are rapidly growing and may become well-known companies in the near future. The vast majority of these growth stocks end up stabilizing at some point and reducing their volatility, so these growth stocks can move into other categories over time. In general, this type of stock belongs to technology companies for which there are high expectations; the only problem is that not all of these companies end up meeting the high expectations that investors have. Therefore, these investments often end up being negative. However, there are many other growth stocks that have achieved their goal and have managed to give investors from all over the world a lot of joy. For example, at its beginning, Amazon was a growth stock, which gradually developed its business model until it became what we know today. Unfortunately, many other promising companies have fallen by the wayside and have failed to meet their targets.

INCOME STOCKS

Finally, we have income stocks, which belong to all those companies that report extremely high annual incomes. In general, these types of companies have a large customer base and a very high sales flow. This gives them very high yearly earnings, so they can meet all the debts and obligations they have to pay. Many investors like to invest in this type of company since they know that these companies will always have enough money to invest in new projects and continue to expand their customer base. And, of course, issue dividends or launch new products (both situations can occur simultaneously). These companies generally belong to the financial sector since they have the greatest liquidity as all their products are based on money. Visa is one of the clearest examples of an income stock that has given its investors very good returns over the years.

Segue: In the next chapter, you will learn everything you need to know about low-risk mutual funds.

16

MUTUAL FUNDS

Investing in a mutual fund is like putting your money on autopilot since you are going to give that money to expert financial professionals who are going to take care of investing that money for you. In other words, a mutual fund gathers money from many people at the same time. It then invests it in financial assets that are supposed to generate profits for those investors. But, of course, although investment funds are managed by professionals, that does not guarantee that you will always obtain good profits since, as we have said many times, the market can sometimes be totally volatile and unpredictable.

The money invested in a mutual fund is managed by a Management Company that specializes in managing different investment portfolios, which may be made up of different securities, such as stocks, corporate and public bonds, real estate assets, international securities, and other funds. The way in which the portfolio is composed is defined in the mutual fund contract; in this way, the investor will make the decision to participate or not according to the preferences that the investor has.

There are 3 types of mutual funds in which an investor can put his money: fixed income, variable income, and mixed-income. Variable-income

funds are aimed at a more risk-oriented investor profile. Variable-income assets are shares of companies or companies that may or may not be listed on the stock market. And as they have greater volatility, they allow higher profits to be obtained. However, as they are titles owned by the company, it implies that the shareholders, or the holders of shares in these funds, may lose the amounts invested in the event of a devaluation of the value of the company or company issuing the shares. Fixed-income funds are bonds or debt obligations issued by states and companies; they are suitable for conservative investor profiles. The return will be closely linked to interest rates' evolution, which is low risk. And the mixed-income mutual funds are intermediate solutions, making a mix of investments in fixed income and variable income. They are very broad, flexible, and are aimed at profiles ranging from those who opt for a certain risk to those close to the riskiest profiles. Diversification is carried out by establishing certain percentages of investment in fixed income or variable income, which will be those that characterize each type of fund. Logically, the higher the percentage of investment in fixed income, the profile of the investor the fund is aimed at will be closest to the conservative profile.

PROS AND CONS OF MUTUAL FUNDS

Undoubtedly, mutual funds have the advantage that they require much less effort and study time for investors. Since you will only have to choose a mutual fund that has had excellent returns in the past, and that's it. Additionally, there are many people who have no idea how to invest or even what a stock is and how they can buy it. For this type of person, mutual funds are excellent and can help them resolve many doubts and problems regarding the possible investments they want to make. However, it should be clarified that investing in mutual funds also has a negative side that is not very pleasant. You will have to pay very high commissions to manage your investments, and in addition, most mutual funds do not exceed the average performance of the market, much less after investors have to pay commissions.

Mutual funds offer many tax advantages to taxpayers, primarily the tax deferral of capital gains—the sale of the shares of a fund will not be taxed. Provided that the amount obtained from them is transferred to another mutual fund. However, many people do not know how to benefit from these tax advantages. That is why the presence of a good accountant in your work team is always recommended so that you avoid having any problems related to taxes.

BEST MUTUAL FUNDS TO INVEST IN

Next, we will review some of the best mutual funds in which you can invest your money. One of them is JPMorgan Chase, which has one of the best mutual funds on the market but charges high commissions. Another one is Fidelity Investments, which manages a portfolio of mutual funds valued at 3.7 billion dollars. Charles Schwab Corporation also has one of the best mutual funds. It has shown that it generates very good returns, despite the fact that you must have a minimum investment amount to open an account there. Lastly, The Vanguard Group and BlackRock are the leaders in the industry, as they pioneered this world of mutual funds and offer the most comprehensive services to investors.

Segue: Inevitably, you will be ready to consider getting into investments that have higher risk but also offer much higher potential gains compared to your low-risk accounts. When the time comes, you need to meet the challenge with some established strategies. And those are what you'll learn in part 4, starting with diversification in the next chapter.

17

DIVERSIFICATION

Throughout this book, we have emphasized the importance of never putting all your eggs in one basket. This means that your investments must be varied and diversified, for if you don't, you will depend on a single sector or a single industry, which can be very risky. Diversifying your investments can be very easy; nevertheless, many people still do not understand the importance of this factor to being successful in investments. All the experts and millionaires in the world recommend diversifying their investment portfolio since that is the only way in which you can be successful when it comes to investing. Diversification can happen in many ways. There are people who prefer to put a little of their money in bonds and a little of their money in stocks; there are other people who prefer to invest in five types of financial assets at the same time. In contrast, other people want to invest in many more financial assets (although this means having less profit) in order to be more protected against volatility.

One of the keys when it comes to diversifying an investment portfolio is to consider the correlation that exists between the prices that make up the portfolio. By correlation, we mean that asset prices rise and fall in equal proportion at the same time. Thus, to prevent the value of the portfolio from falling suddenly, it is crucial to have uncorrelated assets. That is, when some fall, others rise so that they compensate for each other and reduce the general volatility of the portfolio.

Today we have better tools in the markets to improve portfolio diversification. In the old days, if we wanted to have broad equity diversification, we had to buy the individual shares of multiple companies. This entailed a high cost of sales commissions, custody, etc. In recent decades, there has been a revolution in the financial industry with the appearance of exchange-traded funds (ETFs). These allow us to buy shares in baskets of assets with the equivalent of buying a single share. When buying a share of an ETF, our exposure becomes approximately equivalent to the positions held by the ETF. For example, suppose you buy shares of an ETF that replicates the S&P 500; its evolution will roughly coincide with the evolution of the S&P 500.

This further shows that we can replicate a portfolio with around 500 of the best companies in the United States with a single purchase. And also, with lower management fees than traditional funds. In this way, by using a few ETFs, we can obtain a truly amazing diversification. However, it should not be forgotten that it is also possible to achieve proper diversification with traditional funds or more complex instruments, such as financial derivatives.

Diversification is an essential tool to control an investment portfolio's risk. It is, therefore, a necessary aspect for its design and configuration and for structuring the heritage. In addition, regardless of the specific gains that are intended for each market, you should think of diversification as a broader concept and reflect on the impact that any fluctuation in your portfolio can have on your assets as a whole.

IS IT HARD TO BE DIVERSIFIED?

Not at all. There are many people who believe that building a diversified portfolio is difficult, but the truth is that it is pretty simple. To do this, you can make a list of your favourite financial assets. Afterwards, you decide what percentage of the money you are willing to invest and how much you want to put into each of them. In this way, you will be able to organize the structure of your investment portfolio, and you will be able to decide which ones to start investing in first. The important thing is that whatever your strategy is, you should always be diversified.

While the investing strategy is not complicated, some people find it challenging to research and thoroughly investigate the financial assets in which they should invest in order to have a solid portfolio capable of withstanding even the worst financial crises. Of course, these things are not achieved in a single day since to have a truly diversified portfolio, it is necessary to acquire a lot of experience in the market and accumulate profits over time. And get to know the most profitable financial assets much better that are appropriate for you. Over time, you will learn to identify which financial assets are best for you, as well as all those that will benefit your portfolio, both in the short and the long term.

Diversification doesn't just work for novice investors; every good investor in the world makes sure they have a diversified investment portfolio since they know the many risks involved in having all their eggs in one basket. Of course, those experts often specialize or focus more on some specific assets, like real estate, stocks, mutual funds, or any of the other financial assets you learned about in this book, but they always look for ways to diversify each of their investments.

Temporal Diversification

Temporal diversification is about buying stocks periodically in small amounts. That way, you avoid entering the market at an inappropriate time and getting an average of stock prices. With temporary diversification, the aim is to average the purchase prices: you will sometimes buy at a high price and other times at a low price, resulting in a reasonable average price.

Economic Sectors Diversification

The instruments of companies from different sectors help minimize the risk of volatility in the investment. In general, different stages or cycles can be detected in an economy which, in turn, can favor some sectors more than others. In other words, in expansion, a rebound is expected in sectors such as consumption, construction, or retail. Accordingly, having diversification by economic sectors expands the possibilities of obtaining better returns on an investment.

Geographic Diversification

Another option is to have a well-diversified investment strategy with stocks and/or investments in different companies in different countries. In this way, the expected returns are linked to each country's economic growth expectations. At this point, it is advisable to invest in countries such as the United States, Germany, France, and emerging economies such as Mexico, with an encouraging growth scenario.

Segue: In the next and final chapter, you'll learn a strategy that has been used by some of the world's most successful investors.

18

DOLLAR COST AVERAGING

Dollar-cost averaging is one of the most basic but most effective strategies when it comes to investing. When we talk about dollar-cost averaging, we refer to the strategy where a person invests the same amount of money from time to time, regardless of the volatility of the market at that time or the macroeconomic situation of the country. For example, suppose you choose to invest an amount of $1,000 every month. Every month you will have to automatically invest that amount of money for this strategy to work. Of course, this strategy has some flaws, since by always investing the same amount of money and on the same day or on the same date continuously, it is likely that sometimes you will invest money in financial assets that are a bit expensive or overvalued. However, investing in this way will allow you to always have an exact date and amount of money to invest. Which is one of the things that cost people the most, and therefore many do not end up persevering in the world of investments. Therefore, dollar-cost averaging is one of the most recommended strategies for novice investors since it is very easy to apply and allows you to have a practical guide on when and how to invest every month.

On the other hand, suppose you do not want to do all these calculations manually. In that case, you can do them by using some of the platforms that allow you to automate these processes. And they will instantly tell you what the ideal amounts and dates are for you to invest your money according to your own goals, which is what really matters.

Of course, you should know that adjustments are always necessary when carrying out this type of investment strategy. That is, at first, your strategy may be based on investing a specific amount of money. But, later, as your portfolio grows and your objectives may change, it is likely that you will have to modify the amount of money that you invest every month. There will come a time when that amount of money you are investing is too little. In contrast, it may be that you no longer need to invest so much money monthly because the effects of compounding have already made your portfolio big enough. The point is that it is always important to review and modify the amounts you invest, at least annually. So that it is much easier for you to reach your goals.

What happens with many people is that they start investing using dollar-cost averaging but neglect to modify the amounts they invest. As a result, your goals today may not be exactly the same as what you will have tomorrow. This is why it is always important to make the necessary modifications and thus optimize your strategy.

PROS AND CONS OF THIS STRATEGY

There are many benefits to the dollar-cost averaging strategy. One of those advantages is that you will be able to invest in an orderly manner and on a specific date every month. This will give you much more peace of mind since, otherwise, you would have to always be thinking about how much you are going to invest and what financial assets you are going to invest in. Instead, through this strategy, you will simplify this entire process, and you will only have to worry about remembering that date you chose to invest every month. However, this strategy has the disadvantage that your objectives can change, as well as the amounts you are willing to invest, so this strategy often has to be modified as time goes by. Of course, this is not such a serious thing since that strategy can be changed in a few minutes. The important thing is that these modifications do not occur every month. As one of the main characteristics of this type of strategy is that you must maintain consistency throughout the process so that it is truly worthwhile. Otherwise, it is likely that this strategy will not work for you. That is why you should evaluate if this strategy is the most suitable to meet your objectives or whether you should consider other types of strategies when investing in order to obtain better results.

CONCLUSION

At the beginning of this book, it is possible you did not know many of the terminologies and issues related to the world of investment. Not everyone does, and that is why people should focus on learning about the world of investments as soon as possible. Without a doubt, today's investment world is open to everyone, unlike in the past, where only financial experts or high-society people could freely invest in the market. However, many people today do not invest their money, not because they cannot, but because they do not know how to do it. This means that people should try their best to learn as much as possible about how the world of investing works, not waste any more time.

As you have seen throughout this book, one of the most important things people should do is put their money to work since that is the only way they can start generating passive income and thus be well-prepared for retirement and build wealth. We are all going to reach retirement age at some point, but only people who have put together a diversified portfolio as soon as possible are going to be able to enjoy all those golden years without having to worry about money. The problem is that there are many people who reach the age of retirement without emergency funds, without savings, and without any type of investment. Therefore, the important thing after reading this book is not only that you stay with all those theoretical aspects, but it is also imperative that you put all that theory into practice and start taking advantage of the rights of compounding and the world of investments. This is to also ensure that you live the life you want without worrying about money. Choosing the right investments involves you assessing your risk tolerance along with other factors such as your age and the amount you can start investing with. It also requires the know-how, personal discipline, and suitable strategies.

People often get frustrated when it comes to investing because they think it's too difficult or they just don't have the knowledge to do it. At the same time, no one likes to risk their money, and many people never dare to invest because they believe that if they do, they will lose all their money quickly. That is why throughout this book, we focus on explaining in detail the operation of each financial asset in which you can invest safely and make your money start working for you. Of course, you may not be an expert initially, as success is achieved through time and experience.

However, you must remember that patience is key in the world of investments and that if you are not patient, you will not be able to see how your money multiplies, and you will not be able to plan your financial future the way you would like. Each of the financial assets that we have been reviewing throughout the book is accessible and does not have many barriers to entry. Best of all, most of them can be acquired by just using your cell phone in the comfort of your home, so that even that will not be a problem or an excuse for you not to invest your money. Investing can be extremely risky and time-consuming, but it doesn't have to be that way because it the most powerful way to build wealth and be financially stable. With the right strategies, you can significantly mitigate the risk and optimise your investments with just a few minutes of attention given to them each day.

It may be a bit scary at first because, as you have learned in this book, no investment is entirely risk-free. However, little by little, when you gain experience, you will realise that investments are much more straightforward than people often think and that you just have to know how to choose the right ones. So, are you ready to start on this wonderful journey to financial freedom? If your answer is yes, then pick the right funds and start investing your way to making profits.

Please kindly leave a review after reading.

REFERENCES

Caplinger, D. (n.d.). *Investing in Bonds: A Beginner's Guide*. The Motley Fool. https://www.fool.com/investing/how-to-invest/bonds/

Financial, Z. (n.d.). *The Importance of Time in the Market vs Timing the Market*. Www.prnewswire.com. https://www.prnewswire.com/news-releases/the-importance-of-time-in-the-market-vs-timing-the-market-301113822.html

Gravier, E. (2021, June 25). *Here's where experts recommend you should put your money during an inflation surge*. CNBC. https://www.cnbc.com/select/where-to-put-your-money-during-inflation-surge/

Hall, J. (2020, July 1). *How to Invest 100 Dollars*. The Motley Fool. https://www.fool.com/investing/how-to-invest/how-to-invest-100-dollars/

Hancock, J. (n.d.). *Should I Invest in Stocks or Bonds? | John Hancock*. JohnHancock. https://www.johnhancock.com/ideas-insights/investing-in-stocks-vs-bonds.html

Here's why time in the market is more important than market timing. (n.d.). Merrill Edge. Retrieved May 25, 2022, from https://www.merrilledge.com/article/focus-on-time-in-market-not-market- timing

How to Invest in Stocks: A Step-by-Step for Beginners. (n.d.). NerdWallet. https://www.nerdwallet.com/article/investing/how-to-invest-in-stocks

How to Start Investing: A Beginner's Guide. (n.d.). Ramsey Solutions. https://www.ramseysolutions.com/retirement/how-to-start-investing

Oswald, M. (n.d.). *Why does time in the market matter more than timing*. Www.-motilaloswal.com. Retrieved May 25, 2022, from https://www.moti laloswal.com/blog-details/Why-does-time-in-the-market-matter-more-than-timing../1769

Treasury Bonds: A Good Investment for Retirement? (2022, January 2). Investopedia. https://www.investopedia.com/ask/answers/041515/treasury-bond-good-investment-retirement.asp